D0399356

The Queens of England

The
Queens of England

Barbara Softly

BELL PUBLISHING COMPANY
NEW YORK

For Alan

This edition is published by Bell Publishing Company,

a division of Crown Publishers, Inc.,

by arrangement with Stein and Day, Inc.

a b c d e f g h

BELL 1979 EDITION

Manufactured in the United States of America

Library of Congress Cataloging in Publication Data

Softly, Barbara.
The queens of England.

Bibliography: p. 128
1. Great Britain—Queens—Biography.   I. Title.
DA28.2.S63 1979   941'.00992 [B]   79-19463
ISBN 0-517-30200-4

Contents

Queen Elizabeth II – with Garter sash (*portrait by Peter Grugeon, Camera Press*)

Introduction

The king was in his counting-house
Counting out his money;
The queen was in the parlour
Eating bread and honey . . .

Not all the wives of the kings of England spent their time eating 'the bread and honey' of happiness. Some would have made better rulers than their husbands. Some meddled destructively or unwisely with their husbands' lives and governments; some had to fight for their own rights and those of their children; some used their energies in founding colleges and churches and supporting charity; some grasped eagerly all the riches that they could lay their hands on; some found their lives unhappy, fruitless and frustrated.

Being queen, the consort of the king, has always counted as a life of service — to the king and to his people. As 'servants' of the public, in the public eye, most of them deserved, and still deserve, a great deal of gratitude.

Matilda of Flanders

Born?
Daughter of Baldwin V, Count of Flanders
Married 1053 William, Duke of Normandy (later William I)
Queen 1066 on his accession as William I
Died 1083. Buried Caen, Normandy
Children:

> *Robert, afterwards Duke of Normandy, who tried to win from Henry the*
>   *English crown and was imprisoned*
> *Richard, died young*
> *William Rufus, William II*
> *Henry, Henry I nicknamed Beauclerk*
> *Cecilia*
> *Constance*
> *Adelaide*
> *Adela, mother of Stephen, King of England*
> *Agatha*
> *Matilda*

When the wealthy Matilda of Flanders was first asked in marriage by William, Duke of Normandy, she promptly refused him, and some highly-coloured tales were spread about. Some said she was already married; others that there was a closeness of blood of which the church would not approve; another story was that she was deeply in love with a fair-haired Saxon called Brihtric and was only waiting for him; the final and most interesting reason was that Matilda, in William's presence, had referred unwisely to his illegitimacy. It was also said that William had been so angry with her that he had waylaid her on her way from church, flung her to the ground and given her the beating she deserved.

Later on, William asked again and was accepted, either because Matilda was attracted by a man of spirit who was so close to the English throne or because she knew what it was like to be turned down herself:

Brihtric had refused to marry her and had sailed back to England. Apparently Matilda never forgot the slight, for years later when William invaded the country, the Saxon's lands were confiscated, the nearby city of Gloucester lost its charter and Brihtric was thrown into prison, where he died or was murdered.

At the time of William's invasion, England was not an isolated island suddenly to be overwhelmed by enemies from overseas. There had been busy traffic for many years to Europe and beyond. The wealthier Saxons crossed backwards and forwards with amazing frequency, visiting the courts of kings and dukes where they often married the sons and daughters, or found refuge from wars in their own country. Edward the Confessor, the Saxon king whose death led to the Norman invasion, had a Norman mother and was largely brought up at the Norman court; he had half-promised his throne to his cousin William of Normandy. The most important Saxon in the country, outside the royal family, was Harold, whose sister was married to Edward and whose father had been the great Earl Godwin of the West Saxons. Harold held so much power during the latter part of Edward's reign that he was expected by the English to be the childless king's heir. In 1063 Harold had the misfortune to be shipwrecked on the Normandy coast; he was immediately captured and his freedom only obtained by a ruse whereby he promised to help William become the next king of the English. When Edward died, naming Harold as his successor, Harold naturally felt that his promise by trickery was no longer valid and he had himself crowned as king.

William of Normandy prepared his battle fleet and, for her part in the invasion, Matilda gave her husband a ship for his own use called the *Mora*; still wealthy in her own right, Matilda provided on the prow a golden figure of a boy, holding to his lips an ivory horn, his other hand pointing prophetically towards England. In 1066 the fleet sailed and in October, at the battle of Hastings, Sussex, Harold, the last of the Saxon kings, was killed. It seems that the main reason for his defeat was that his army was already tired and shrunken: for weeks Harold's soldiers, the best infantry in Europe it was said, had been up in the north of England fighting off an invasion from Norway. Hurriedly marching south, they were no match for William's massive force.

Matilda's first visit to England, when she was crowned two years later, was brief. Like most conquered people, the English were not going to accept defeat easily in spite of William's brutal methods to put them down – his destruction of towns and villages, his curfew (*couvrefeu*, cover the fire,) at 8 o'clock each evening which made it impossible for rebellious meetings to be held after dark – and Matilda found it wiser to return to Normandy with her children. With two countries to control and growing sons who objected openly to their father's jurisdiction, William had to delegate some of his power to his wife.

In Normandy, Matilda showed her capabilities by ruling the Duchy for her husband; but she also sided with her eldest son, Robert, in his rebellion against his father. Robert knew that he was his father's heir in Normandy but not in England, and as that honour had been reserved for his younger brother, William Rufus, his jealousy flared into civil war. Matilda drew upon her riches to help him and when Robert was eventually sent into exile arranged for a messenger to carry money and letters. The messenger was caught and William would have had him blinded had not Matilda's friends helped him to escape and sent him to a monastery under the protection of the queen. Matilda's generosity to the churches and the needy in Normandy was well known and she had no scruples about robbing English abbeys in order to support them.

Although she was provided for as queen of England – twelve pence a day for each of her 100 attendants, forty shillings for food at table, lamp oil and fuel given by the City of London – Matilda spent little time there and it is not likely that she had any part in the making of the famous Bayeux tapestry. It is far more probable that this beautiful piece of needlework was made by the Saxons in Kent. The Normans were great admirers of Saxon craftsmanship, particularly their work in gold, jewels and embroidery, and Odo, William's half-brother, may have ordered the tapestry for display in his abbey at Bayeux in Normandy to celebrate the story of the Norman Conquest. It depicts Westminster Abbey, built by Edward the Confessor, Edward's death, William's preparation of ships for the invasion, Halley's comet streaking across the sky on its seventy-five year orbit, the battle of Hastings and the death of Harold. It can still be seen today in Bayeux.

The importance attached to the beautiful work of the English is shown by Matilda's will in which she left to the Abbey of Caen, which she and William founded soon after their marriage, her tunic 'worked at Winchester by Aldoret's wife'. Other than gold cups and trappings for her horses she had little to leave, for she bequeathed all her land to her fourth son, Henry Beauclerk.

Matilda died at Caen aged fifty-one. In spite of their obvious disagreements she must have had a moderating influence on her husband.

After her death, William, one writer said, 'became a thorough tyrant' and the conquered English suffered accordingly.

Matilda of Scotland

Born 1080
Daughter of Malcolm III of Scotland
Married 1100 to Henry I
Queen 1100 to 1118
Died 1118
Buried at Westminster
Children:

William, who was drowned
Matilda, who became Empress Matilda and fought against Stephen for the English crown
Richard, who was drowned
Mary, who was drowned

Matilda's mother was Margaret, a Saxon princess, granddaughter of Edmund Ironside. On the Norman invasion she had taken refuge in Scotland where she married Malcolm Canmore, King of Scotland. To her small daughter she first gave the Saxon name of Edith, but to please the Normans this was afterwards changed to Matilda.

When Matilda's parents died and relations with the Normans were easier, Matilda, her sister Mary and five brothers were taken to England, the boys to the court of William Rufus and the two girls, at their mother's wish, to Romsey Abbey in Hampshire to be educated. The children of royal Saxon families had always been brought up at Romsey; and the girls' aunt, Christina, was a nun there.

Christina was not satisfied with giving her niece Matilda an excellent education – she wanted her to become a nun and used every effort to influence her. Dire warnings of dangers from brutal Norman barons and William Rufus himself were given; threats, insults and finally blows, in order to force the young princess to take the veil. 'I trembled under my aunt's rod,' said Matilda, years later. 'Whenever I could get out of her sight I flung the veil to the ground and trod it underfoot,' and she gave as her reason her father's wish that she should be married. She must have seemed even more contrary when she steadfastly refused the first two offers of marriage made to her. Apparently she was waiting for the man with whom she had already fallen in love, Henry I of England.

It had been a relief to the English people when William Rufus, second of the disliked Norman kings, was killed in the New Forest and his younger brother Henry came to the throne. Henry had the advantage of having been born in England and when he said he would try to right some of the wrongs of the previous reign and marry a princess of Saxon blood, his popularity was ensured. When he asked Matilda to marry him she immediately consented. The one person who would not consent was Christina. She caused so much trouble by insisting that Matilda was a nun and was therefore unable to marry, that the determined girl wrote to Anselm, Archbishop of Canterbury, asking for his help. He called together an assembly in London, where Matilda was closely questioned about her life in Scotland and at the Abbey.

She must have made a good impression. Not only was Matilda very well-educated with a great love of music, she was honest. She admitted that she had worn the black veil on occasions, partly to please her aunt, partly to protect herself from the unruly Norman barons and marriages that she did not want; but she insisted that all along she had remembered her father's wish that she was not to enter the church. When, at last it was decided that she could marry Henry, Matilda 'received the verdict with a happy smile'. They were married at Westminster on 11 November 1100.

For the English it was a time of comparative peace. Matilda was a good peacemaker herself and was able to write tactful letters to both the Pope and the Archbishop of Canterbury when her husband was not on speaking terms with either of them. As queen, she tried to live among her people the life she had not been prepared to give to the Abbey, perhaps believing that it was better to practise Christianity rather than to think about it. Like her mother, she wore a hair shirt – and went barefoot in Lent, gave food and clothing to the poor and washed the feet of the lepers in London, although Henry did not approve of this last action and more practically she helped build a hospital for them. Possibly her love of giving was a fault, for it was said that she taxed her own tenants too heavily in order to be able to have money for musicians, poets, scholars and churches.

When Henry was abroad looking after his lands in Normandy, Matilda was still as energetic. She had the roads throughout England repaired and new ones made, and once, after she had nearly been drowned at the dangerous ford over the river Lea, a few miles outside London, she insisted that a bridge should be built. There were really two bridges linked by a gravel causeway over the marshes, probably the first stone arched bridges ever to be built in England. Matilda paid for the work herself and saw that there was enough money for the constant repairs. One of them, Bow Bridge, despite many alterations, lasted until 1835, when it was completely replaced.

Matilda died, aged thirty-nine, while Henry was away in Normandy. The people had loved her, for she had restored, so it seemed to them, the Saxon line to the throne. It was said of her later by Robert of Gloucester, that 'the goodness that she did here to England cannot all be here written nor by any man understood'. 'Molde, the good queen' was a fitting epitaph.

Matilda is remembered today by one of the oldest statues in Britain. On either side of the beautiful Norman west door of Rochester Cathedral, Kent, are the figures of Henry and Matilda. Henry carries a church with a steeple in his hands; Matilda holds a scroll and wears her long hair in two plaits over her shoulders.

Adelicia of Louvain

Born 1102?
Daughter of Godfrey of Louvain, Duke of Brabant
Married: (i) 1120 Henry I — his second wife; no issue
*   (ii) William de Albini — seven children*
Queen 1120, until Henry's death, 1135
Died 1151. Buried Alost, Flanders

Henry had loved his first wife, Matilda, and it is not likely that he would have married again had not an even greater tragedy than her death overtaken him. All his children, except the young Empress Matilda who was already married and living in Germany, were drowned in a shipwreck off the French coast.

In November 1120 the court was preparing to sail back to England from Barfleur, France, after having celebrated the marriage of Henry's eldest son, William, and it was William's idea that all the young people should travel together in the fastest ship of the fleet, the *Blanche Nef* — literally, the White Vessel. Henry gave reluctant permission, probably guessing what would be thought of him if he refused. At dusk the party swarmed on board, everyone except William's little twelve-year-old bride, who was sailing with her father-in-law. They were in high spirits, planning to while away the Channel crossing in music, dancing and drinking, for William had seen to it that extra wine had been put on board and he had the foresight not to forget the captain and crew. One person who boarded the *Blanche Nef* was Stephen, William's cousin, the son of his aunt Adela. Stephen took one look at the deck strewn with the merry-makers, remarked that the ship was obviously 'overloaded with foolish, headstrong young people' and refused to sail with them. In darkness, the sails crowding the mast, the tipsy crew bending to the oars so that the *Blanche Nef* should live up to her reputation and beat the other vessels round the point, the ship sped out of the harbour. She struck a rock and sank. Out of the 300 people on board, only one survived.

Henry reached England unaware of the accident and it was several days before anyone had the courage to tell him of it. Ill-tempered and morose as he had become after Matilda of Scotland's death, he now grew so unapproachable that it was hoped a gentle wife and perhaps a new-born heir might save his sanity.

Adelicia was only eighteen at the time of her marriage and she seemed to have everything that Henry's advisers thought he needed: she was beautiful, sweet-natured, calm and home-loving – she had already shown what an excellent needlewoman she was by embroidering a standard for her father, the Duke of Louvain, to carry into battle with him. After her marriage, she showed that even if she had no interest in state affairs, she was fully prepared to be interested in her husband's hobbies. At different times during his reign, Henry had wheedled out of visiting dukes and princes all kinds of strange animals, camels, leopards, lions and even a porcupine to form a zoo at one of his palaces. Apparently, Adelicia was sufficiently anxious to learn about wild animals to have a book especially written for herself on the subject. At the beginning the author wrote –

> 'Philippe de Thuan, in plain French,
> Has written an elementary book of animals
> For the praise and instruction of a good and beauteous woman,
> Who is crowned queen of England, and named Alix.'
>
> (Strickland)

Unfortunately for Adelicia Henry often had to be away from England protecting his lands in Normandy, and during the fourteen years of their marriage she was alone for years at a time. Perhaps it was not surprising that there were no children, and Henry decided eventually to make his daughter Matilda his heir. Empress Matilda, now a young widow, was recalled from Germany to live in England and, much against her will, was forced to marry again – Geoffrey of Anjou, known as the Plantagenet because of his habit of wearing a sprig of broom in his helmet (*planta* – sprig, *genista* – broom). From Matilda and Geoffrey came the Plantagenet or Angevin line of English kings.

It was while Henry was in Normandy in 1135 that he died suddenly, according to the old story of a 'surfeit of lampreys', little eel-like fishes of which he was very fond, eaten after a day's hunting. The consequences for the English people were disastrous. It was civil war for the next fifteen years between the young Empress Matilda and her cousin Stephen, her father's favourite nephew, and all because some of the courtiers at Henry's deathbed maintained that he had changed his mind and pronounced Stephen to be his heir, not Matilda.

Adelicia, with calm and tact, managed to steer a safe course between the pair of them. She went to live at Arundel castle in Sussex, which was part of her dower. There she gave shelter to Empress Matilda on her arrival in the country and when Stephen threatened to attack them, Adelicia persuaded him to let his rival leave in safety because she was only treating her as her stepdaughter and not as a claimant to the throne. Adelicia married again and continued to live at Arundel untouched by the civil wars. She had seven children and her heirs became the well-known Howards and Dukes of Norfolk who have owned Arundel to this day. But, strangely enough, she did not die there. She left her husband, children and home and went back to her own country to become a nun, dying there when she was about forty-eight years old.

Matilda of Boulogne

Born 1103
Daughter of Eustace III Count of Boulogne
Married before 1125 Stephen of Blois
Queen 1135 to 1152
Died 1152. Buried at Faversham, Kent
Children:

Baldwin and Maud, who died young

Eustace, buried at Faversham
William, who lived on friendly terms with Henry II, the son of the Empress
Marie, Abbess of Romsey

Matilda of Boulogne was named after her aunt, Matilda of Scotland, wife of Henry I. As the daughter of the Count of Boulogne and Mary of Scotland, she must have inherited a number of qualities from that strong-minded queen, for she was equally determined and tactful — an ideal partner for Stephen, Henry I's nephew, in his wars against their common cousin, the Empress Matilda, Henry's daughter.

The Empress Matilda had left England as a young child to be married to the Emperor of Germany and it is possible that it was from him and his court that she acquired her haughty ways. Matilda of Boulogne, on the other hand, was just as young when she was brought to England to be educated at Bermondsey Abbey. (The abbey, near London Bridge, grew rich during the following centuries, but all that remains of it now are the names of Abbey Street and Crucifix Lane.) She was married to the handsome, likeable Stephen who, after Henry's children were drowned in the *Blanche Nef*, went everywhere with his uncle; he could hardly be blamed for hoping that, along with the estates in England that were showered upon him, the crown might eventually fall into his lap, too.

Matilda and Stephen had another advantage over the Empress: they actually lived in London, in a castle-like residence called Tower Royal off Cheapside, whereas the Empress Matilda was, no sooner called home on the death of the Emperor than she was packed off unwillingly as the wife of Geoffrey of Anjou. Gossip in England at the time had it that if the handsome Stephen had not been married already, the Empress would gladly have had him — which would have saved a deal of trouble later on. As it was, the unhappy Empress refused to live with her new husband and it was six years before she had a baby son. Whether it was his or not was open to some doubt; no one denied that it could have been Stephen's.

For some years after Stephen and Matilda had been crowned, the Empress personally made no move to claim her throne. It was only after Stephen started having trouble with his barons, and more trouble in Normandy where he was always needed, that she landed in England hoping to gain support. Stephen and Matilda looked for support, too, and found plenty, although many people felt that the Empress, as Henry's daughter, had the better claim. It was when Stephen was finally captured and imprisoned by the Empress, who then called herself the Lady of England, that Queen Matilda came into her own and showed the determination for which her family was famous.

She tried everything within her power to have her husband set free – pleading letters, approaches from powerful barons, even a promise that Stephen and his heirs would give up the English throne and enter a monastery if he could have his freedom. When the Empress still refused, Matilda realised that, against her better nature, she would have to resort to force and gather as many followers as possible to fight her cause. Here the Empress unwittingly helped her, for her bad temper and arrogant manner so put up the backs of Londoners that someone irritably called her 'a niggish old wife' and she and her supporters were chased out of the City. From London to Oxford, Oxford to Winchester, Devizes and Gloucester ran the Empress, and during her flight her strongest general, the Earl of Gloucester, was captured – to Queen Matilda's delight. She treated him well and used him as a hostage for her husband's life, cleverly negotiating an exchange of prisoners, to the annoyance of the Empress.

After Stephen was released, the war went on as before. There is a famous story of how once the Empress was besieged and escaped over the snow-covered fields wrapped in a white cloak. At last she was forced to leave the country, but she knew at the back of her mind that most of the English barons were not prepared to have any of the children of Stephen and Matilda on the throne. That honour was to be reserved for her own son, Henry.

During the brief time of peace, Queen Matilda turned her thoughts to more domestic affairs. She founded the hospital of St Katharine in London and she and her husband founded the abbey of Faversham, Kent. Matilda lived in Canterbury for a while so that she could watch the actual building in progress, and when she died, agéd about forty-five, she chose to be buried in this new church. Stephen was buried there, too, and their eldest son Eustace. Faversham Abbey disappeared when Henry VIII had so many of the monasteries and nunneries in England destroyed, but during excavations in the 1960s the remains of the tombs of Stephen and Matilda were discovered.

Eleanor of Aquitaine

Born 1122
Daughter of William X Duke of Aquitaine
Married: (i) Louis VII of France, 1137
           Divorced 1152, 2 children
           (ii) Henry of Anjou in 1152
Queen on Henry's accession as Henry II of England in 1154 until his death 1189
Died 1204. Buried at Fontevrault
Children:

> *William, died young*
> *Henry, died in his twenties*
> *Matilda*
> *Richard, who became Richard I*
> *Geoffrey, the father of Arthur, who was murdered by King John*
> *Eleanor*
> *Joan*
> *John, who became king.*

It was written of Eleanor of Aquitaine that she was one of the very few women in history who made up for 'an ill-spent youth by a wise and benevolent old age'. If the stories told about her are only partly true, then the Women's Liberation Movement is not an invention of the twentieth century; Eleanor founded it eight hundred years ago.

As a gifted intelligent girl of thirteen, with a love of drama and a marked ability for composing the popular troubadour songs of the period, she was married, with her own approval, to Louis VII of France. Louis was serious-minded and, during the fifteen years of their marriage, not easily able to cope with his wife's enthusiasms and attraction to other men. When Louis planned to go on a Crusade — one of the expeditions by Christian kings to try to win back the Holy Land from the Mohammedans — Eleanor insisted on joining him, not as his wife, but as a combatant. She had already raised a band of women who, lightly armed and mounted on horseback, accompanied her everywhere. She and her followers sent their distaffs in contempt to any nobleman not willing to support the Crusade: as the distaff was used in spinning and was therefore an emblem of womanhood, the action implied cowardice, just as the sending of a white feather implied during World War I.

It seemed to be by mutual agreement and not only because Eleanor had given her husband two daughters and no son and was probably unfaithful to him, that they obtained a divorce (1152). Six weeks later, Eleanor married Henry of Anjou, the son of the Empress Matilda.

Henry could now claim as his own Anjou, Normandy and the rich province of Aquitaine to the south, which his wife had brought him. For anyone in Europe he was a formidable enemy, especially as he intended to uphold his right to the throne of England as well. He made one or two sorties into England, but when both Stephen and his son Eustace died suddenly, Henry took his chance. In 1154, he, Eleanor and their baby son William landed in England for their coronation, at which Eleanor became the queen of the first Plantagenet or Angevin King of England. The ceremony was one of the most magnificent the English had ever seen, Eleanor loved rich silks and velvets embroidered in gold, not only for herself but for the churchmen as well. The church having forbidden men to wear their hair long, Henry wore his short with a moustache and no beard. His little short cloak of the type fashionable in Anjou so amused the English that they nicknamed him Courtmantle. England prospered with the Aquitanian connection, particularly in the wine trade and shipping.

The fact that Eleanor was twelve years older than her husband did not promise well for the marriage, especially when she discovered that Henry already had another lady, whom he had promised to marry, hidden away at his palace of Woodstock. This was Fair Rosamund, after whom the lovely old striped red-and-white rose, Rosa Mundi, was named. It is possible that Rosamund did not know that Henry was married on his return to England, for on realising the situation she entered a nunnery.

During the next twenty years, Eleanor had four more sons and three daughters. She helped to arrange the 'marriage' of her seven-year-old Richard to the three-year-old French Princess Alice. Little Alice was brought up in England, but she never became Richard's wife. There were some strange stories circulating that Henry himself would have liked her for his bride when she was older in spite of the difference in their ages. Henry's frequent unfaithfulness to his wife, his favouritism towards his youngest son, John, his unwillingness to give his elder sons any recognition, together with the uncertain temper inherited from the Empress Matilda, led him into serious trouble. Although as king he restored order throughout the country and instigated the beginnings of the English jury system, he could neither control his temper nor his family. His furious shout for someone to rid him of the 'insolent priest' Thomas à Becket, led to the murder of his one-time friend in Canterbury Cathedral and Eleanor, acting as regent in Normandy and Aquitaine as she had frequently done during her married life, willingly joined her sons in open rebellion in 1172. Prince Henry, the heir, supporting his father, died fighting his brother Richard. When the rebels wisely fled to the French court, Eleanor, with her usual ingenuity, dressed up as a man and tried to escape, too. She was caught, brought back to England and kept prisoner, probably in the palace of Winchester and allowed out only on public occasions. At the same time, Fair Rosamund died in her convent and Eleanor was unjustly blamed for her death.

When Henry died sixteen years later in 1189, Richard I, the new king, ordered his mother to be released, and made her regent of England so that she could govern while he was out of the country at the Crusades. Eleanor, now sixty-seven, showed that she had not lost her old spirit; she went through England making herself known to the people; she freed anyone who had been wrongly imprisoned under the harsh Norman laws which Henry had brought back, and pardoned those who had been outlawed for hunting in the royal forests. Although she was given full powers to punish those who had been her gaolers, she did not take advantage of this, but she kept the thirty year-old Princess Alice under guard for some time before letting her return to France.

The next years were as busy as the previous ones had been dull. Eleanor governed England well during her son's long absences. She travelled across Europe to meet the Princess Berengaria, who was to become Richard's queen and she tried to quell the troubles that arose all too easily in her provinces. One of her main troubles was with her youngest son, John, who had to be prevented from seizing the English crown when his brother was taken prisoner in Europe.

Eleanor outlived her son, Richard I, and was able to see the first five years of John's disastrous reign. When she died aged eighty-two, she was buried near Henry at Fontrevrault Abbey in France. Most of the early Plantagenets were buried in this abbey; it is now a prison.

Eleanor's strong individuality is shown by the way in which she sometimes signed her letters: 'Eleanor, by the grace of God, humbly, Queen of England' or 'Eleanor, by the wrath of God, Queen of England'.

Berengaria of Navarre

Born?
Daughter of Sancho VI of Navarre
Married 1191 to Richard I and queen until his death in 1199
Died after 1230. Buried at Espau
No issue

Berengaria's shadowy figure contrasts with Richard I's known flamboyance and good looks. Tall, golden-haired, courageous, a man who loved fine horses and jewelled saddles, his clothes were as colourful as himself. Silver brocade, rose, scarlet and gold made up his tunics, cloaks and caps. Berengaria remains a half-forgotten Queen of England who never visited her husband's country. The Cunard Line named one of their fastest Atlantic passenger ships after her in 1920, but no one else seems to have remembered her.

That she was graceful, dark-haired and intelligent seems to have been accepted, as she was the daughter of Sancho the Wise of Navarre. It was at a tournament in her own country that she and Richard are supposed to have met. Immediately fascinated by her quiet beauty, Richard wished to marry her, although he had been engaged to Alice of France since a child. When that engagement was eventually broken off, it was decided that Berengaria should travel from her home to Sicily, where Richard might find time away from his latest Crusade in the Middle East to marry her. Most of Richard's life was spent in fighting the Saracens in the effort to win back the Holy Land for Christians; as he was only able to spare ten months of his ten-year reign for visiting his own kingdom, his reluctance to meet his bride was not remarkable.

Berengaria travelled with Richard's mother, Eleanor of Aquitaine, the redoubtable dowager queen who acted as one of England's regents during her son's absence. In Sicily it was learned that Richard was planning a pilgrimage and also the forthcoming siege of Acre in Palestine, and no time could be wasted in marriage festivities. At Acre he was sure of victory, Berengaria could sail in his fleet of 100 ships and be wed there.

The intrepid Berengaria and her ladies embarked, but one of those sudden storms for which the Mediterranean is famous sprang up, the fleet was scattered, ships were wrecked, lives were lost and for five days Richard scoured the area for his missing bride. He found her, and everyone else on board, frightened but unharmed, sheltering off the coast of

Cyprus, too terrified to land having seen the fate of the other ships which had been plundered by the unfriendly Cypriots. With typical impulsiveness Richard attacked the island, drove the Cypriots and their leader out of the capital of Limasol into the mountains and, to celebrate his victory, married Berengaria within the week. At the same time she was crowned Queen of England and of Cyprus.

The placing of the Cypriot leader's young daughter in the care of Berengaria gave rise to a number of rumours about Richard, but as he was known to prefer the company of men to women and fighting to settling down, it is not likely that there was much truth in them. Afterwards Berengaria went with her husband to Acre, but following Richard's further successes in the Holy Land they parted and travelled separately into Europe, where Richard was captured and imprisoned in Austria. Later, after his discovery and ransom, he made a triumphal entry into England and throughout his kingdom. Berengaria did not see him again for four years. She apparently waited quietly in Italy and Aquitaine.

When he went back, after a serious illness during which grave accusations were made against his way of life and unsavoury companions, it is said that Berengaria accompanied him everywhere and was with him when he died of an arrow wound at the siege of the castle of Chalus.

As dowager queen Berengaria was entitled to a yearly income from the flourishing tin mines in Devon and Cornwall. Under King John, Richard's heir, who blamed the situation on 'the wickedness of his barons', she did not receive a penny. Under Henry III some of the debts were paid and she was able to found a Cistercian abbey at Espau in France. There she lived until her death, some thirty years after Richards.

Avisa of Gloucester

Born 1167?
Daughter of the Earl of Gloucester
Married: (i) *Prince John, 1189 (later King John)*
divorced 1200, no issue
(ii) *Geoffrey de Mandeville*

Isabella, Hadwisa and Avice are variations of her name. She was the daughter of William of Gloucester and with her two sisters, Amicia and Mabel, was heir to her father's vast estates.

In 1176, at nine years old, she was betrothed to Prince John and married him in 1189, bringing him immense power in the west. As both John and Avisa were great grandchildren of Henry I the marriage was frowned upon by the church. Ten years and many mistresses later, when John was king and had been crowned – a ceremony in which Avisa took no part – John was only too glad to remember the church's disapproval and the fact that he had no legitimate children. The marriage was annulled on the grounds of consanguinity and Avisa was given a new husband, Geoffrey de Mandeville, Earl of Essex, who had to pay about 20,000 marks for the honour of marrying the king's former wife. John, naturally, kept her inheritance.

Isabella of Angoulême

Born 1187?
Daughter of Aymer Count of Angoulême
Married: (i) John, 1200 (his second wife)
*   (ii) Hugh de Lusignan*
Queen 1200–16 on John's death
Died 1246. Buried at Fontrevrault
Children:

   Henry, later Henry III
   Richard, Earl of Cornwall
   Joan, wife of Alexander II of Scotland
   Isabella, wife of Emperor Frederick II
   Eleanor, wife of the Earl of Pembroke and then wife of Simon de Montfort,
     founder of the English Parliament

Isabella was about thirteen years old and betrothed to a local baron, Hugh de Lusignan, when she met John in Aquitaine. Whether it was a love-match or purely political, any difficulties in the way of the marriage of Isabella and the English king were easily overcome. John divorced his first wife, Avisa, and Isabella, at the prospect of becoming a queen, broke off her engagement.

On returning to England, John insisted on a second coronation so that his young bride could be crowned with him. They embarked upon a life of idle luxury – rarely rising before midday, taking frequent baths and eating enormous meals. John delighted in spending the money his father had saved and, according to the household accounts, had cloaks and girdles studded with diamonds and sapphires, white gloves which bore a ruby on one hand, a sapphire on the other, cups of silver and a wand of gold. By comparison, Isabella's wardrobe was plain – a cloak with nine bands of grey fur, another of scarlet linen, rolls of green and grey cloth, four pairs of boots and material for a pair of purple sandals.

Isabella was disliked in England as queen and she has been referred to as a 'beautiful and mischievous woman', but how much she influenced her husband in his ruthlessness is not known. John did not hesitate to imprison her himself when he felt the need arose. When his own barons began to object to the harsh laws he was introducing, John ordered them to send their children to the court to wait upon Isabella as pages and attendants. One mother refused, saying that she could not trust her children to a man who had murdered his own nephew – this referred to the sixteen-year-old Arthur of Brittany, who had been nearer the throne than John. John had the whole family seized. Isabella was asked to intercede on their behalf but not even the gift of 400 white cattle could save them; the parents and five children were shut in one of the many castles John used for such nefarious purposes and starved to death.

Eventually the English barons forced John to Runnymede to sign the charter they had drawn up, the famous Magna Carta, a document intended to curb the monarch and safeguard the freedom of Englishmen for all time. John signed the parchment, though the episode so enraged him that while progressing through the countryside he took a petty delight in setting fire to every house where he had stayed a night. As he continued to break his word, the English invited the French to invade the country and John fled northwards, misjudging the tide while hurrying across the Wash and, a famous incident, losing the crown jewels in the water. He took shelter in a nearby abbey where he was heard to mutter in one of the violent tempers for which he has gone down in history that he would 'make the ½d loaf cost a shilling before the year was out'. Rumour had it that the monks were so angry at this threat of increasing his revenues at their cost that they poisoned him; more likely his death soon afterwards was due to a fever caught in the marshes.

On his death Isabella had to act quickly to safeguard the interests of her young son Henry, then only nine years old. He was proclaimed king at Gloucester where, the crown having been 'lost in the Wash', or so legend asserts, the enterprising churchmen set on his head a gold collar belonging to the queen. It was arranged that the country should be governed by a Protector until Henry III came of age. No one suggested that Isabella should be regent, and before the year was out the unwanted queen-dowager took herself back to Angoulême and married the man to whom she had originally been engaged. Her influence over him seemed no more stabilising than it had been over John, and his country was soon plunged in war with France; the bitter affair came to a head when Isabella was accused of having tried to poison the king of France. Innocent or not, no one except the church would give her shelter and she fled to the abbey of Fontrevrault. There she is supposed to have been hidden in a secret room for the rest of her life.

Eleanor of Provence

Born?
Daughter of Raymond Berenger IV Count of Provence
Married in 1236, Henry III, and queen until his death, 1272
Died 1291 at Amesbury and probably buried there although heart at Newgate, London
Children:

Edward, later Edward I
Edmund, Earl of Lancaster
Margaret, who married Alexander III of Scotland
Beatrice
Katherine, Richard, John, William and Henry who all died young and were buried in Westminster Abbey.

Eleanor was another queen for whom the English had little liking, although neither she nor Henry had the unpleasant characteristics of John and Isabella. Henry may not have been a strong king but he was kindhearted and cared for his people enough to give to the poor. On one occasion he had the royal children weighed and their weight in silver given to the poor of Windsor.

Eleanor, called 'La Belle' because of her beauty, was the gifted daughter of the equally gifted Count of Provence. Theirs was a country known for its music, literature and poetry and no harm was done to the English court by having a little of this culture introduced. Henry himself loved beauty and had the walls of his palace painted with pictures of Saxon history. In spite of the Norman Conquest most of the later kings were anxious to keep their Saxon links. Henry and Eleanor named their eldest son after Edward the Confessor and Henry rebuilt the eastern end of Westminster Abbey as a shrine for the saint.

Beautiful buildings and a beautiful wife needed money, and when Eleanor came to her coronation no one objected then to the vast sums spent on her clothes and jewellery. The streets were swept and the people watched spellbound as over 300 horsemen, each carrying a gold or silver goblet, rode to the banquet. But admiration and pride in a lovely young queen turned to annoyance and open rebellion when it was realised how many friends and relations Eleanor had brought from Provence. She had great influence over her husband and he was easily persuaded to favour these friends and relations with jewels, money and high positions. Eleanor, too, tended to take advantage of her rights as queen. Since Saxon times the toll money, paid on the cargoes unloaded at the quay known as Queenhithe, in London, had always gone to the queen, and now Eleanor made sure that as many ships as possible, especially those carrying valuable cargoes of wool and corn, unloaded at her wharf. Even Henry made the Londoners pay for his little pleasures by taxing them 4d a day for the upkeep of a white bear in his new menagerie at the Tower.

Here are a few of Eleanor's expenses during a period of nine years:

For linen, feeding the poor, kitchen, servants and upkeep of horses	£6,618
Silks, dresses, stockings for her ladies	£180
Buying horses, clothes for the family, shoes and saddles	£1,691
Secret gifts and private alms	£4,017
Jellies, spices, apples, pears	£252

Eleanor's unthinking behaviour, together with the taxes levied to support wars in her lands abroad and the favours showered on her family, brought matters to a head and the country plunged into civil war. Simon de Montfort, the husband of Henry's youngest sister, Eleanor, led the rebels who demanded from the king less extravagance and a fairer government of the kingdom. During one riot, when Eleanor and her ladies were trying to escape down the Thames in a barge, they were pelted with sheep's bones, rotten eggs and the loose stones from London Bridge while the mob screamed 'Drown the witch! Drown the witch!'

The civil war brought fierce fighting, particularly at the battle of Lewes in Sussex. This battle Henry and his son Edward lost, mainly because Edward was so angry at the way the Londoners had treated his mother that he chased the enemy too far and was trapped himself. Henry and Edward were not only defeated by Simon de Montfort; they were taken prisoner and Eleanor had to flee abroad. Edward managed to escape, rallied his loyal forces, won a great battle at Evesham in Worcester and reinstated his parents. Nevertheless England profited by Simon de Montfort's victories, for it was he who formed the basis of parliament as it is known today by sending representatives from every large town to meet in London.

During Henry's long reign of fifty-six years, the English had been forming themselves into a nation – a fact which may have had some bearing on Eleanor's unpopularity. A proclamation at this time had to be read in three languages – Latin for the well-educated and the Church; Norman-French for the court and anyone who had come from abroad; Saxon for the ordinary people, whose dialect varied up and down the country. The graceful Early English and Gothic style of architecture came into being under Henry's patronage.

As in his will Henry had appointed Eleanor regent, when he died in 1272 she called together a council of peers and prelates to name her son as the new king, Edward I. The large sum of money which she was allowed as queen-dowager Eleanor took with her when she retired to the nunnery at Amesbury in Wiltshire. She lived for another nineteen years and left enormous debts for her son to pay.

Eleanor of Castile

Born?
Daughter of Ferdinand III of Castile
Married 1254 to Edward, Prince of Wales (later Edward I)
Queen 1272, until her death in 1290
Buried at Westminster
Children:

   John ⎫
        ⎬ *died in infancy*
   Henry ⎭

28

Alphonso, named after Eleanor's brother, died aged twelve years, buried in Westminster Abbey.

Edward, later Edward II

Eleanor

Joanna, married Gilbert de Clare, Earl of Gloucester

Margaret, married Duke of Brabant

Mary, became a nun

Elizabeth, married as her second husband Humphrey de Bohun Earl of Hereford

Isabella

Beatrice

Berengaria

Blanche

Only Edward and Mary outlived their parents for any length of time.

Eleanor was probably ten and Edward fifteen when they were married and, as it was usual for such a young princess to continue her education, her father-in-law, Henry III, had a home prepared for her at Guildford Castle in Surrey. There he insisted that her room should have glazed windows, a raised hearth, a chimney, a wardrobe and a small extra room where she could pray. Edward continued his education by competing in tournaments abroad whenever he could until he was called back to England by the outbreak of civil war some years later.

When Eleanor grew up she seems to have spent most of her married life following her energetic, handsome husband on Crusades, or up and down the country in wars with the Welsh and Scots. Edward's constant battling earned him the nickname of 'The Hammer of the Scots'. When someone pointed out to Eleanor that she could easily lose her own life by accompanying her husband into such dangerous places, she replied that it did not matter: 'nothing should come between those whom God hath joined' and 'the way to Heaven is as near, if not nearer, from Syria as from England or my native Spain'. Both Edward and Eleanor appear to have been down-to-earth people. When they were on a Crusade and news came to them first that their two small boys at home in England had died, and then that Edward's father had died too, Edward broke down only on hearing of his father's death: his explanation to his surprised companions was that God could give him more sons, but that no one could give him another father.

Eleanor and Edward returned to London for the coronation at Westminster; for a fortnight, country people and townsfolk were feasted in hurriedly constructed wooden buildings which were 'open at the top to let out the smoke of cooking'.

As queen, Eleanor accompanied her husband on his next campaign into Wales and it was at his newly built castle of Caernarvon in the north that her fourth son was born. The old story is that the Welsh had told Edward that they would only accept a ruler who had been born in Wales and could speak neither French nor English. When Edward showed them his little son, who naturally had the necessary qualifications, and called him the Prince of Wales, the Welsh knew that they had been tricked. Eleanor, at least, had the good sense to employ a Welshwoman, Mary of Caernarvon, as the baby's nurse. The room where the young Edward was born is small, dark and narrow. An eighteenth-century book describes what was supposed to have been his cradle: it was about three feet long, of rough, carved oak on rockers and crowned with two birds. In spite of the discomforts of Edward's Welsh castles – another child, Elizabeth or Isabella, known as the Welshwoman, was born at Rhuddlan – Eleanor enjoyed beauty and luxury. She used tapestries to decorate bare walls and had gold and silver cups, jugs and ewers, silver knives and forks, combs and looking-glasses and a silver bodkin in a leather case.

Altogether she had thirteen children, four boys and nine girls, but she did not welcome the Church's representations that she ought to be able to spare one of her daughters for God by letting the child enter a nunnery. Eventually reluctant permission was given for the ten-year-old Mary to go to the convent at Amesbury, where the dowager queen Eleanor of Provence was still living.

Only a year later, while following Edward north on his march into Scotland, Eleanor was taken ill in Lincolnshire. On hearing the news, Edward forgot the Scots and the Welsh: Eleanor meant more to him than anything else and he rode south to be with her. By the time he reached her she was dead. Grief-stricken, he had her body embalmed and accompanied it on the slow journey back to London. Wherever the travellers rested, Edward had a cross erected in his wife's memory – Eleanor Crosses – the last one being at what is now known as Charing Cross in London, a name supposedly derived from the French, which Edward spoke – *chère reine,* dear queen. Three of the original thirteen crosses remain, at Northampton, Geddington and Waltham Cross in

Hertfordshire.

Eleanor's memorial in Westminster Abbey is perhaps the most beautiful that Edward could have given her. She lies on her tomb, her hair falling in soft waves over her shoulders, her left hand holding the strings of her cloak. The inscription, 'Here lies Eleanor . . . daughter of the King of Spain. . . .' is written in Norman-French.

Margaret of France

Born 1282?
Daughter of Philip III of France
Married 1299 to Edward I (his second wife) and queen until his death in 1307
Died 1318. Buried at Christ Church, Newgate, London
Children:

> *Thomas, Earl of Norfolk, whose family later were linked with that of Adelicia at Arundel*
> *Edmund of Woodstock, Earl of Kent*
> *Margaret and Eleanor, who both died young*

Edward was over forty years older than his second wife, who was only seventeen when she married him. According to all the writers of the time, Margaret or Marguerite, the younger daughter of the king of France, was a woman who had no faults. Throughout the remainder of Edward's reign, the royal accounts and the stories told about the queen show that she was loving, giving and not entirely afraid of her fiery-tempered Plantagenet husband. On several occasions she paid the debts of people who owed him money and saved the lives of others that he would have had put to death. 'We pardon him solely at the intercession of our dearest consort, Marguerite, Queen of England' was recorded when she pleaded for the life of the goldsmith who had made the crown for Robert Bruce, the man the Scots had chosen for their ruler to fight against Edward.

Edward was still bitterly at war with the Scots and was determined to subdue them in his lifetime. They, under their leader William Wallace, defeated the English at Stirling and then were defeated themselves only a year later. Wallace was betrayed, captured, taken to Westminster in chains and executed. At the time, Margaret was celebrating the investiture of her husband's eldest son as the Prince of Wales and perhaps it was distress at the terrible cruelties that she saw inflicted by both sides which made her try to influence Edward's revengeful nature.

When Margaret first came to England, before she started accompanying Edward on his campaigns, she lived at the Tower of London and had to stay there when the court was in quarantine for smallpox, brought into the city by the Crusaders. She began her reign quietly, for although Edward had a crown made for her, his wars were proving too expensive for her to be allowed a coronation as well. At least he named his own ship, perhaps a state barge, after her – *Margaret of Westminster*; and Margaret herself had a personal chaplain, John of London, who wrote down the doings and a description of her elderly husband. 'Edward,' according to John, 'never wore his crown after his coronation . . . and went about in the plain garments of a citizen', actions of which not everyone approved. He was nicknamed Longshanks because of his height and ability to leap so easily into the saddles of his horses.

Edward's last expedition to try to defeat the Scots was taken when he was seventy. The strain was too much for him and he died near the Scottish border. Margaret first saw that the new king, Edward II, her stepson, was married to her niece, Isabella of France, and then she retired to Marlborough Castle in Wiltshire. She died there, aged thirty-six, and was buried in Grey Friars Church in London. There is a small effigy of her on the tomb of John of Eltham, her husband's grandson, in Westminster Abbey.

Isabella of France

Born 1292
Daughter of Philip the Fair of France
Married 1308, to Edward II
Queen 1308–27
Died 1358. Buried at Christ Church, Newgate, London
Children:

  Edward, who became Edward III
  John of Eltham, died aged nineteen
  Eleanor
  Joanna, wife of David Bruce, King of Scotland

Isabella was the daughter of the king of France and the Queen of Navarre, and the niece of Margaret, second wife of Edward I. Not only was she a very royal young girl, but a very beautiful one: by the time she was thirteen, when she married Edward II, she had earned the title of Isabella the Fair. Yet years after her death, Gray, the poet, spoke of her as 'She-wolf of France, with unrelenting fangs', referring to the tenacity with which she plotted the downfall and murder of her husband.

It is almost impossible to believe that Edward II was the son of Edward I and Eleanor of Castile; strong physically, he had 'no dignity, no self-respect and talked too much'. Even during his father's lifetime, in spite of careful upbringing, he was frivolous and extravagant, obsessed with per-verted friendships for other men – mostly of low character – and with little concern for the kingdom he was to inherit or the powerful nobles surrounding him; on coming to the throne he recalled the favourite, Piers Gaveston, whom his father had dismissed. The prospect for the country was grim and fraught with ill-omen for the young girl he was about to marry. The coronation festivities of Edward and Isabella were nearly wrecked by his behaviour with Gaveston and the money, gifts and time he should have lavished on his bride went openly to his favourite.

Although Isabella brought with her from France gold and silver gob-lets, spoons, dishes, furs, linens and eighteen dresses, she was soon with-out money of her own, due to Edward's extravagance, and she wrote long letters to her father complaining about her treatment. Edward remained reckless in bestowing affection, wealth and power on Gaves-ton and in making enemies in his own court. The French king began to give the discontented barons, led by Thomas of Lancaster, his secret sup-port. The result was civil war in England yet again.

Among the royal accounts which show some of Edward's extrava-gances are orders for tasselled boots for himself, flame-coloured silk for making cushions, silver bowls for New Year gifts, presents of money to foreign messengers who had brought him a box of rose-coloured sugar, and a gift of twenty pounds to three members of the court for 'dragging the king out of bed on Easter morning'.

For years Isabella attempted to be loyal to her husband, pleading with him 'with tears in her eyes' to stay with her for the birth of their first child – a request which he refused. During that time, probably feeling her loneliness, she adopted a little Scottish orphan boy. Young Thoma-line, as he was called, was fed and clothed and sent to live in London with Isabella's French musician and his wife, who continued to bring him up at Isabella's expense.

Edward, disobeying his father's last wish that he should conquer the Scots completely, left the Scots, under Robert Bruce, to ravage the north of England unhindered. The rest of England was in the grip of a three-year famine; even the royal family went without bread. Finally disaster struck again on the borders of Wales. Here, the English were more successful and captured one of the ringleaders, Roger Mortimer, who was imprisoned in the Tower of London. The Tower was also one of the residences of the royal family, a safe place in troubled times: Isabella was there too. Somehow Isabella and Mortimer met, and from that moment Edward was a doomed man. Mortimer escaped from the Tower and fled to France.

Two years later, Isabella persuaded Edward to let her go to France, taking their thirteen-year-old son. She made out she was asking help from her French relatives for Edward against his rebellious barons; in reality she went to join Mortimer and plan how they could overcome Edward and place his son on the throne. When Isabella returned to England with support for the barons, Edward was taken prisoner. Previous prisoners of Isabella and Mortimer had been treated cruelly; the king was no exception. He was humiliated and forced to give up the crown, with which his young son was immediately crowned as Edward III.

Young Edward may have been king but the country was ruled, very badly, by Isabella and Mortimer, who hoped that their unwanted royal captive would die in the appalling conditions in which he was kept. Unfortunately Edward had the magnificent Plantagenet constitution; he was taken to Berkeley Castle in Gloucestershire and murdered. It was said in the village nearby that 'many a one woke and prayed to God for the harmless soul which that night was departing in torture'.

As soon as Edward III was old enough to throw off the power of his mother and Mortimer, he had Mortimer imprisoned and executed and Isabella had to give up the money she had taken for herself as queen-dowager. She was sent to live at Castle Rising in Norfolk, a castle which had once belonged to Queen Adelicia's second husband. There, with ladies to wait upon her and regular visits from her son, she spent a happy retirement, and in later years would visit other parts of the country.

She died aged sixty-three, and there is some doubt where she is buried, although the Church of the Grey Friars, Newgate, of which she was a benefactor, claims the remains of both Isabella and her daughter Joanna.

On the tomb of her second son, John of Eltham, in Westminster Abbey, is a small figure of her, with those of her husband and Margaret of France.

Philippa of Hainault

Born 1314
Daughter of William, Count of Holland and Hainault
Married 1328 to Edward III, queen until death in 1369. Buried at Westminster
Children:

Edward, the Black Prince, father of Richard II
Lionel of Antwerp, Duke of Clarence, who was nearly seven feet tall
John of Gaunt (because he was born in Ghent) Duke of Lancaster. Father of Henry IV
Edmund of Langley, Duke of York
Thomas of Woodstock, Duke of Gloucester
two Williams who died young
Isabella, married into the Cecilly family
Joan, died of the plague aged fifteen
Mary, married into the Montfort family
Margaret
Blanche

Philippa is one of those few characters from the past who, in Shakespeare's words from the 'Merchant of Venice', shone 'like a good deed in a naughty world'. The world of the Middle Ages was a grim place of constant disease — lack of sanitation affected everyone and the court moved from castle to castle, palace to palace as each building became too unpleasant to live in. Famine, early death, war, intolerance, cruel sport and cruel punishment were an accepted way of life. Philippa, one of the four daughters of the Count of Hainault, with her loving nature, humility, compassion and strength of character managed to lighten this darkness while she was Edward's queen. When she died, 'beloved of God and all men', Edward, as with so many of the Plantagenets, was completely broken and the better side of his nature, together with the better side of court life, came to an end.

Philippa was barely fourteen when she and Edward were married at York. They had previously met in Hainault when Edward was taken

Philippa of Hainault and Anne of Bohemia (*by Jean de Liège*)

there by his mother, Queen Isabella, and Philippa had shown her affection for the young prince then. The coronation, two years later, was an inexpensive affair because the Dowager Queen Isabella had already spent Philippa's dowry and her son's wealth in continuing her wars in England and France. When the chamberlain who had officiated at the ceremony asked, as his right, for the three small basins in which the queen had washed her hands, for her shoes and the bed in which she had slept, Edward said he could take everything except the bed and for that he would have to pay 100 marks. But in spite of the obvious poverty of court and country, the English could enjoy themselves. Edward was deeply interested in King Arthur and the Knights of the Round Table – he founded the Order of the Garter because of this interest – and he staged grand tournaments and joustings at which his own knights could compete against each other. At one tournament at Cheapside in London, held in honour of the birth of their first child, Edward, the Black Prince, the special stand provided for the queen, her ladies and members of the court collapsed; Philippa and most of the spectators were in considerable danger and Edward, with typical fury, demanded to know the names of the carpenters and ordered them to be put to death. It was Philippa who saved their lives.

Again it was Philippa who saved the lives of the men of Calais when Edward had besieged the town into submission. Edward had continued the war against France, a war which was to continue for a hundred years, pawning the queen's crown to help pay for it, and the town of Calais had held out for almost a year; starving, turning to dogs and rats to keep themselves alive, the brave people at length gave in, hoping that the enemy would be merciful. Instead, Edward, angry that so many of his own men's lives had been wasted in the siege, at first wanted to put the whole town to the sword. He changed his mind to demanding that six of the leading citizens must appear before him, ropes round their necks ready to be hanged. For Philippa, the injustice was too great: the famous story tells how she went down on her knees in front of everyone and pleaded for the men's lives. Edward, probably seeing that a refusal could only make himself look foolish and unchivalrous, reluctantly let them be spared. Edward's other victories during the Hundred Years' War were the sea battle at Sluys, and the battles of Crécy and Poitiers.

Philippa was brave enough during Edward's absence abroad to tackle the Scots, who were invading the north of England. Riding a white horse, she went herself to the battlefield and encouraged the army before the fight began. The court ladies were fascinated by all the attention to military affairs and soon began wearing small jewelled daggers at their waists and large, square headdresses similar to their husband's helmets.

Philippa's energy and intelligent mind were not satisfied with tournaments, wars and having babies – she had twelve children altogether – and she was able to turn her attention to settling the people from her own country in England as weavers of wool. It had been said of the English that they had plenty of wool, but were so ignorant that they did not know what to do with it – 'any more than the sheep that bore it'. Philippa's Flemish weavers settled in Norwich and soon a flourishing clothmaking industry was started there to be visited frequently by the queen when Edward was visiting his mother at Castle Rising. From the cloth trade to coal was only a step and on Philippa's estates there were disused coalmines: these were re-opened and England began to exploit its two great assets, coal and wool.

When Philippa was taken ill at Windsor and knew she was dying, she made several requests to her husband: that he would fulfil all she had promised to do and pay any of her debts; give money to churches in England and Europe which she had already promised to them; look after her servants; and in due course be buried at her side. Her tomb is in Westminster Abbey and the effigy of her is supposed to be a good likeness. Edward spent an enormous amount of money on her memorial although little of the original now remains.

Anne of Bohemia

Born 1366
Daughter of Emperor Charles IV of Bohemia
Married 1382 to Richard II and queen until her death in 1394. Buried at West-minster
No issue

'Good Queen Anne' was the name by which Richard II's queen was known. She was not beautiful, but as Richard had particularly asked for a kindhearted bride and Anne's family was related to Philippa of Hain-ault, she seemed the right choice for Philippa's grandson.

Richard, son of the Black Prince, who was Edward III's eldest son, was not born in England, but in Bordeaux: he was often spoken of as Richard of Bordeaux, and as his early years were spent there his upbringing was probably not the same as if he had been reared in England. He became king at ten years old, on the death of his grandfather, and it was obvious to his ministers that life was not going to be easy with his powerful uncles and cousins keeping a watchful eye on the throne.

The disturbances at the beginning of his reign were not so much on the Scottish and Welsh borders, but with the discontented ordinary people, whose resentment at heavy and unfair taxation erupted into the Peasants' Revolt of 1381. The peasants formed themselves into a rough army which ravaged, pillaged and burnt with the wild abandon which was usually turned against them. Under their leader Wat Tyler they marched to London, where young Richard, aged fourteen, bravely rode to meet them and listen to their demands. Wat Tyler was suddenly struck down and the ugly scene which could have followed was prevented by Richard riding among them, saying he would be their leader and try to help them. But his efforts on their behalf were soon after reversed by his ministers, and the rebellion was put down with great harshness.

It was soon after these events that Anne, daughter of the Emperor of Bohemia, arrived in England to be married at Westminster, and it was her pleading which prevented further cruelty and punishment. For these small acts of kindness and for later ones, the ordinary people loved her.

Anne's arrival at Dover was heralded by the strange phenomenon of a giant, swelling wave which immediately wrecked the ship in which she had sailed, a disaster looked upon as a sign of ill-omen. With her, Anne brought a large number of Bohemian followers and two odd fashions: a new kind of side-saddle for ladies to use on horseback, and the most enormous headdress seen in England, about two feet high and wide, shaped like a horned moon, draped with soft, filmy gauze or net. When English ladies copied her, the church looked upon the creation as sinful partly because it outshone even their magnificent headdresses or mitres. Richard and the men at court were not to be outdone in extravagance: the toes of their pointed shoes, 'Cracowes', now grew so long that they had to be fastened to their legs with silver or gilt chains.

New fashions were symptomatic of the new ideas seeping into the country. For a long time fresh ideas about religion had been growing in Europe and England. The pope in Rome was the accepted head of the church, but people were beginning to want to think for themselves, to loosen the hold of priests and monks. In England, John Wycliffe had been trying to reform and simplify Christian beliefs. His writings had spread to Bohemia from where they now returned with the Bohemians Anne had brought with her. Anne, it was known, could read the Bible in three languages, and Wycliffe's followers saw no reason why the Bible should not be translated from Latin into English for the ordinary English people to understand. John Wycliffe's wandering preachers, the 'Lollards' spread through the country, and it is believed that Anne gave them some encouragement and protection.

Anne and Richard were together at their palace of Sheen, in Surrey, when she became ill with the plague. Within three days she was dead. Richard was completely shattered by her death; she was only twenty-eight and they had been married eleven years. In his grief he cursed the palace and ordered it to be pulled down. Anne's funeral was magnificent; wax was sent from abroad for candles and torches; the citizens of London were clothed all in black with black hoods to take their place in the funeral procession. Later, Richard was able to think about her memorial in Westminster Abbey and he took the unusual step of having his own effigy made to lie alongside hers on the tomb, their hands clasped in affection. On their clothes were stamped the badges of both their royal houses—the white hart and the broom-pod for Richard, the two-headed eagle and the lion for Anne.

Isabella of Valois

Born 1389
Daughter of Charles VI of France
Married: (i) Richard II in 1396 (his second wife)
*   (ii) Charles, Count of Angoulême, in 1406*
Queen from 1396 to 1399 when Richard was deposed
Died 1409. Buried at Blois, later at Paris
Children:

  None by Richard II
  One daughter by Charles of Angoulême

Isabella was the daughter of the king of France. When asked if she would like to be queen of England, she replied that she would—'for then I shall be a great lady'. She was seven years old.

It was obvious that Richard, having had no children by his first wife Anne of Bohemia, would have to marry again. Whether he showed tact or guile by his choice will never be known. By marrying Isabella he could end the war with France; and if he was still grieving for his beloved Anne, he knew it was not possible for the small girl to take her place as his wife for a number of years. Richard and Isabella were married at Calais and 'the little queen', as she was called, was crowned at Westminster a year later, so many people crowding on the narrow London Bridge to see her that nine were crushed to death. She was apparently very fond of Richard, who had visited her frequently, taking her presents. The only time he upset her was when he ordered her French attendants to leave the country because they were too expensive to keep.

Behind Richard, wherever he went, stalked the figures of his uncles, John of Gaunt and Thomas of Gloucester, and John's son, Henry Bolingbroke. Sometimes they sided with each other against the king, sometimes one or other sided with the king, but all the time they knew Richard was a weak ruler and sooner or later they would be able to overthrow him. The last gift Richard gave Isabella was a dog, perhaps as a companion, for he knew instinctively that he would never see her again. He surrendered to his enemies. gave up the crown and was imprisoned in Pontefract Castle, Yorkshire, where he either starved himself to death or was murdered. Isabella was kept a prisoner while the king of France demanded the return of his daughter. Henry Bolingbroke, now Henry IV, finally agreed and ordered Isabella to be brought before him. The little dowager queen refused to acknowledge the new king or to speak and she remained a silent, sullen figure in black throughout the meeting.

To return home to her parents must have been a bitter blow. She is known to have been very unhappy and even more unhappiness followed when she was told a few years later that she was to marry her own cousin. He was younger than she was and Isabella wept throughout the marriage ceremony.

Isabella died when she was twenty, only a short while after her first baby was born.

Mary de Bohun

Daughter of Humphrey de Bohun Earl of Hereford
Married Henry Bolingbroke (later Henry IV) 1380
Died 1394. Buried at Leicester
Children:

Henry, Prince Hal, who became Henry V
Thomas, Duke of Clarence
John, Duke of Bedford
Humphrey, Duke of Gloucester
Blanche
Philippa

Mary and her sister Eleanor, two of the richest young girls in the country, were the sole heirs of the Earl of Hereford and at an early age were both married, Eleanor to Thomas of Woodstock, brother of John of Gaunt, Mary to Henry Bolingbroke, Duke of Lancaster, son of John of Gaunt. In a family sense, Eleanor was then the aunt of her sister Mary.

Mary died a few years before Henry became king.

Joanna of Navarre

Born 1370?
Daughter of Charles d'Albret, King of Navarre
Married: (i) John IV of Brittany
(ii) in 1403 Henry IV (his second wife)

Queen from 1403 until Henry's death in 1413
Died 1437. Buried at Canterbury
Children:

  By first husband four sons, four daughters
  By Henry IV, no issue

Joanna was another queen who had an uncomfortably stormy crossing to England. Her ship should have sailed into Southampton from France, but instead it was blown off course by terrible winds for five days until it finally landed in Cornwall.

Joanna, perhaps, was well-used to storms of a different nature. She was the daughter of the king of Navarre, Charles the Bad, who was actually so ferocious that on one occasion Joanna and her sister were held hostages for his good behaviour. At sixteen Joanna was married to the Duke of Brittany, known as 'the most quarrelsome prince in Europe'. She, however, coped with his ill-temper and difficult nature, giving him eight children before he died and she was left a widow.

By that time, Joanna had already met Henry Bolingbroke, Duke of Lancaster, whose first wife, Mary, had died, and it appeared that the pair of them were determined to marry in spite of the objections of the church: Henry had sympathies with John Wycliffe's teachings which were against the beliefs of Joanna's pope. Joanna obtained permission from the Church for the wedding by not divulging the name of the bridegroom. She then sailed for England with her two youngest daughters and, having landed in Cornwall, travelled to Winchester where she and Henry IV were safely married.

Their arrival in London was greeted with the usual celebrations and processions; a band of musicians had been especially hired from Suffolk to play; the mayor, aldermen and sheriffs put on their robes and everyone else wore 'a red hood on his head'. An old picture shows the new queen and her husband seated watching the jousting at a tournament held in their honour. Joanna is wearing the large headdress which was fashionable at the time and at her side are tasselled cushions for her to rest her arms.

Joanna managed to get on very well with her step-children, particularly Henry's eldest son, Prince Hal, so often in trouble with his father. But after her husband's death, when young Henry V was once more at war with France, the storms gathered again. Henry V was, un-

Joanna of Navarre (*electrotype*)

fortunately, fighting Joanna's relations, and it must have been hard for her to rejoice with the English at a victory like Agincourt, while in her heart mourning the overthrow of many of her own family.

The matter did not rest there. Unpleasant rumours about the dowager queen claimed that she was trying, by witchcraft, to poison Henry V. Without any warning or a chance to defend herself, she was sent to Pevensey Castle in Sussex. Pevensey can boast that it is one of the few castles in England which has been in constant use for the defence of the country since Roman times. Even during World War II it was patched up and pill-boxes to hide machine-gun posts were built on the Roman walls. After four years in prison, Joanna was allowed her freedom. She lived quietly, through the reign of Henry V and into that of Henry VI, dying when she was about seventy. Her death was noted with another of equal interest—'died Queen Jane, Henry IV's wife. Also in the same year died all the lions in the Tower, which was nought seen in no man's time before—.'

She was buried in Canterbury Cathedral alongside Henry IV. Her effigy shows that she must have been a very attractive woman.

Catherine of Valois

Born 1401
Daughter of Charles VI of France
Married: (i) in 1420 Henry V
*   (ii) Owen Tudor*
Queen from 1420 until Henry died in 1422
Died 1437. Buried at Westminster
Children:

> *Henry VI*
> *By Owen Tudor, three sons and one daughter*

Catherine was the youngest sister of Richard II's 'little queen' Isabella. In fact, Henry V had high hopes of marrying that small widow himself, but had to turn his attention to Catherine instead.

Catherine's and Isabella's parents may have been odd – their father was unbalanced and their mother took little notice of her children – but they were the king and queen of France, and Henry desperately wanted to regain all that the previous English kings had lost and rule France as well as England. He intended to achieve this either by marriage or conquest. His offer to the French king for Catherine's hand demanded as her dowry, two million crowns, and the return of Normandy and the territory once belonging to Eleanor of Aquitaine. Insane or not, the French king had sense enough to reject such an enormous price for allowing his daughter to become queen of England.

Henry declared war and Catherine, it seems from writers of the period, was not unduly upset by the terrible bloodshed suffered by her countrymen on her behalf. Possibly she took a little pride in the fact that she was worth fighting for, as she is known to have been eager to marry the handsome English king. Following many defeats, the French agreed to the marriage, although peace was not really restored and the bride of nineteen spent the first months after the wedding accompanying Henry from battlefield to battlefield. Eventually they set sail for England and the coronation.

As the coronation took place in Lent, the banquet afterwards consisted of fish — stewed eels, jelly coloured with columbine flowers, cream of almonds, fried smelt, lobster, baked lampreys, sturgeon with whelks, roasted porpoise and other dishes decorated with hawthorn leaves and red haws. By midsummer, Catherine was expecting her first baby. Henry was superstitious and before he returned to France warned the queen against having the child at Windsor Castle. Catherine disobeyed him and the baby, Henry, was born at Windsor. On hearing the news Henry said:

I, Henry born at Monmouth, shall small time reign and much get;
But Henry of Windsor shall long reign and lose all.

Within ten months the prophecy showed signs of coming true; the baby's father was dead and he was proclaimed Henry VI. Catherine took him to his first opening of Parliament seated on her knee, but she had no part in his coronation when he was seven years old. The youthful dowager queen mysteriously disappeared from public life and the country heard very little about her.

Catherine was a beautiful widow of twenty; her baby was the responsibility of his guardians and the regents of the country and it is hardly surprising that she turned her attentions to another matter. This was Owen Tudor, a Welsh soldier whom she had met at court. For several years Catherine and Owen managed to keep their friendship secret except from a few close acquaintances, until the young king's guardians became suspicious of his mother's relationship with a commoner. By then it was too late. Catherine was apparently married, with a growing family whose births had been carefully concealed. Owen Tudor was arrested and sent to Newgate – he managed to escape; Catherine took refuge in Bermondsey Abbey where, already ill after the birth of another baby and broken by her separation from the children and Owen, she died.

Even in her will she made no mention of her marriage, but Henry VI, when he was old enough to understand how his mother had been treated, saw that his young stepbrothers were brought up carefully. Edmund, the eldest, was married to Margaret Beaufort, the heiress of John of Gaunt and their son became Henry VII.

There is a full-length wooden effigy of Catherine in Westminster Abbey.

Margaret of Anjou

Born 1430
Daughter of Duke of Anjou
Married 1445 to Henry VI and was queen until he was deposed in 1461, and
*   again in 1470–1 until he was murdered*
Died 1482. Buried in Angers Cathedral
Children:

*   Edward, killed at the battle of Tewkesbury aged eighteen*

Although Margaret was the wife of Henry VI and therefore the queen of England, she can hardly be the traditional 'queen in the parlour'. From the time she married Henry until she was forced to leave the country many years later, she took an active part in the affairs of state. Too active many would have said, because she would like to have ruled the country on her own. She was the intelligent, strong-minded daughter of gifted parents who had led an unsettled life in Anjou for many years. It seems hard now to put too much blame on a young queen for the events in England which led to the Wars of the Roses. What girl of fifteen, as Margaret was at the time of her marriage, thrust into a foreign country, married to a dreamer, with few friends to advise her and those probably the wrong ones, almost forced to take the government out of her husband's hands, would not make mistakes? Henry VI was a man who should not have had to be king at that troubled period of English history. He had none of his famous father's warlike spirit. He hated fighting and unpleasantness and would have preferred to spend his time reading, studying or living in solitude like a monk.

The marriage was not popular with the people. Margaret was French and the English regarded the French as their hereditary enemies. If they had to have a French queen, they might have accepted one who brought them French lands and money, but Margaret was penniless and only brought an uneasy peace between the two nations. As the English did not want peace their energies found outlet in creating war among themselves, internecine feuding which rumbled continuously in the background.

Margaret, as so many other continental brides, had an unhappy crossing to Southampton. She was ill, seasick or with something described as 'smallpox' though she recovered within a few days. Henry, as was often the case with English kings, had no money, either for the wedding or the coronation, and had to get the crown jewels out of pawn by pawning many of his own. Someone thoughtlessly gave the royal couple a lion for their wedding present, which added considerably to their expenses when they had to take the animal up to the Tower of London with them after their marriage at Titchfield Abbey, near Southampton.

Henry gradually took less and less part in state affairs and Margaret was forced to make important decisions for him. At that stage Henry's relatives were not over-worried that the queen had so much power; the king was childless and they were his heirs. But when Henry became insane like his grandfather and Margaret had a baby, they took a different view and the Wars of the Roses broke out in earnest. Henry was descended from Edward III's third son, John of Gaunt, Duke of Lancaster and John's first wife. His house of Lancaster, with the red rose as their emblem, fought the house of the Duke of York – who bore the white rose. Through his marriage to a descendant of John of Gaunt and his third wife, and his descent from Edward III's fourth son, Edmund of Langley, the Duke of York maintained he had the better claim to the throne.

The Earl of Warwick, spoken of in history as 'The Kingmaker', was a supporter of both sides and successively married off his daughters to whichever member of the royal family seemed most likely to come to the throne. Isabel married the Duke of Clarence; Anne was married firstly to Edward, Prince of Wales and then to Richard III.

Margaret made great efforts to rally support for Henry and his son Edward. In victory she made a cruel enemy, but in defeat she had courage and stamina, for it was then that Edward IV, as Yorkist king, admitted he was more afraid of her than of all the princes of the house of Lancaster put together. From time to time Henry was captured and Margaret managed to get him freed. At other times she, her husband and child were hunted, half-starving, through the countryside, living on 'herrings and no bread' for several days. After the terrible defeat of the battle of Hexham, when 'King Henry was the best horseman of the day, for he fled so fast no one could overtake him', Margaret, with the ten-year-old prince and a few followers, fled in another direction. Within a few miles they were caught, not by the Yorkists but by a marauding band of robbers, who stripped them of all their valuables, jewels, cloaks, furs and dresses. Margaret was dragged on her knees before their leader, and with a drawn sword at her throat pleaded for her life, telling the man who she was and imploring him not to harm her or the child. The story goes that at that moment his companions started quarrelling and fighting over their spoils, distracting the leader's attention. In a flash Margaret seized Edward and they sped away. By nightfall both of them were ravenously hungry, their remaining clothes in rags and they were lost in the depths of Hexham forest. Suddenly, in the moonlight, a menacing form rose out of the undergrowth. Terror-stricken, Margaret blurted out that it was little use the man robbing her for that had already been done, and she had nothing to lose but her life. If he took that, she hoped he would be merciful enough to spare her son because he was the future king of England. She had met not one of the former robbers, but a lone outlaw, and his actions have gone down in history. Either he believed Margaret or he was sorry for her, because he took the tired prince in his arms and led the way to his cave on the banks of a nearby stream. After two days he found her friends and guided them all to a place of safety from where they eventually set sail for France.

Margaret stayed in France for seven years; Henry was a prisoner in England, and Edward IV had been proclaimed king, but with so many troubles of his own arising in the kingdom that she began to have hopes of regaining the throne for her son. She returned to England and, with the help of Warwick the Kingmaker, saw the Prince of Wales married to the earl's youngest daughter. The happiness was shortlived. The Lancastrians were defeated once more at Barnet, and final defeat came at Tewkesbury where young Edward was killed – or possibly deliberately murdered. In fact it was not long before his father Henry suffered the same fate, and the widowed Queen Margaret was made a prisoner for five long years. At the end of that time, the French king paid the first instalment of her ransom and she was allowed to go home, having first signed a document on which she renounced all claims to anything in England and was not even permitted to say that she had once been queen and the wife of Henry VI.

If Margaret's intelligent brain and other talents had come at a more peaceful time in English history, she would probably have worked for the betterment of the country. As it was, she still managed to help the woollen and silk trades by encouraging women to take part in the manufacturing. She also founded Queen's College, Cambridge (Henry founded King's College). She died aged fifty and was buried in Angers Cathedral.

Elizabeth Woodville

Born 1437?
Daughter of Sir Richard Woodville
Married: (i) Sir John Grey
*   (ii) In 1464 Edward IV, and was queen until his death in 1483*
Died 1492. Buried at Windsor
Children:

> *By first husband, two sons; one was the ancestor of Lady Jane Grey*
> *By Edward:*
> *Elizabeth, who married Henry Tudor (Henry VII)*
> *Mary, died young*
> *Cicely*
> *Edward, became Edward V, murdered in the Tower aged thirteen*
> *Richard, murdered in the Tower aged eleven*
> *Anne*
> *Katherine*
> *Bridget, became a nun*
> *Margaret, died aged nine months*

Elizabeth's mother was a Luxemburg princess whose family did not approve of her marriage to an ordinary English squire called Woodville. Whatever their feelings may have been, the princess and her squire were happy and brought up a family of seven sons and six daughters of whom Elizabeth or Isobel— the names were the same — was the eldest. Elizabeth grew up with a natural instinct for mothering, protecting and helping her many brothers and sisters, which made her unpopular later in life.

She was first married to a staunch supporter of the Lancastrians, Sir John Grey, and became a lady of the bedchamber to Henry VI's queen, Margaret of Anjou. But Sir John was killed at the battle of Barnet, and when the Yorkist Edward IV had had himself proclaimed king, all the estates of Elizabeth's husband were taken from her and she was left penniless. Undeterred, the attractive widow — whose pale golden hair was so long that it reached her knees — set about trying to see the new king for herself, to persuade him that she needed some means of support for her children. She did not ask for an audience at court but, apparently, waited until Edward was hunting in the forests near her mother's home in Northamptonshire and waylaid the king alone. Under an oak tree, which was known as the Queen's Oak until the nineteenth century, she approached, a son clinging to either hand, and made her request. Edward was fascinated, as he usually was by beautiful women and not always because he wanted to marry them. Elizabeth made it plain to him that although she knew she was not good enough to become his queen, she was far too good to become anything else. At dawn one May day, they were married, with only four other people present so that the wedding could be kept a secret as long as possible. Edward knew that his actions would have little approval from court or family.

After the shock of the king marrying a commoner had passed, and Elizabeth had been crowned at Westminster, she set about helping those brothers and sisters even in her mind. With Edward's co-operation, for it seemed she was able to twist him round her little finger, wealthy marriages were arranged for most of them: most notoriously she partnered off her twenty-year-old brother with a rich old lady of eighty. Edward was still occupied with the Wars of the Roses, fleeing from the country when the Yorkists were in turn defeated, so Elizabeth busied herself with her babies. After having three girls, she was forced by the dangers of the war to take refuge in the sanctuary at Westminster for the birth of her fourth child. So little Edward V was born in the poorest circumstances. The Abbot of Westminster gave what comforts he could; Master Gould, a local butcher, saved the queen from starvation by sending in 'two muttons and half a beef' every week; Mother Cobb acted as nursemaid.

Elizabeth gained a certain popularity by her courage under such conditions and when she and Edward were finally again victorious, they were able to afford luxurious conditions at their own court at Windsor. There were pleasure gardens and vineyards; indoor games and dancing; the guest rooms were hung with 'white silk and linen cloth' and all the floors were covered in carpets; cloth of gold and white curtains hung on the four-poster beds. After taking a bath, we are told the guest was given green ginger and spiced wine to drink. Unhappily for Elizabeth her pleasures ended as soon as her husband died and she was left completely unprotected. Edward's interests had led him to encourage William Caxton and the first printing press in England; Elizabeth had refounded and helped the college at Cambridge begun by Margaret of Anjou, but neither of these were of any importance beside the great question of who should be the next king.

Lawfully, it should have been the thirteen-year-old Edward, but Elizabeth was so worried by the events taking place in the country that, once more, she took refuge in the sanctuary at Westminster. With her went Edward's brother Richard and all his sisters. Edward V was duly proclaimed king, but was taken into the care of his uncle, Richard of Gloucester, who demanded that his other nephew should be taken into his protection too, in order to keep Edward company in the Tower. The horrified Elizabeth protested that the boy was not well and, in any case, left alone in each other's company, the princes, like most brothers, would probably quarrel; but she had to give in. The boys died, their bodies not being discovered for two hundred years; it is generally believed they were murdered by agents of Richard of Gloucester, who proclaimed himself Richard III, although more recently Henry VII has come under suspicion.

Elizabeth, the once dowager queen, was now referred to simply as Dame Elizabeth Grey. Again she set about trying to help her family, her daughters who could so easily suffer the same fate as their brothers. On the one hand she tried to arrange a marriage between Elizabeth, the eldest, and Henry Tudor, the supporter of the Lancastrians, on the other, she tried to negotiate with Richard III for their safe conduct out of Westminster. In the long run, her double-dealing was of little help to herself. She went, either for safety or because she had nowhere else to live, to Bermondsey Abbey and remained there in semi-retirement until she died, aged about fifty-five; in her will she said she had nothing to leave to anyone except her blessing. She was buried without any ceremony beside Edward IV at Windsor, during the reign of Henry VII and her daughter Elizabeth of York.

Anne Neville

Born 1456
Daughter of Richard, Earl of Warwick
Married: (i) Edward, Prince of Wales, son of Henry VI
*   (ii) in 1474 Richard, Duke of Gloucester, who became Richard III in*
*   1483*
Died 1485. Buried at Westminster
Children:

*   Edward, died aged eight*

Anne must be the only queen in English history who worked as a kitchen-maid in order to escape an unwanted marriage. Unlike Cinderella in the fairy tale, her story has no happy ending.

Anne was the second daughter of the Earl of Warwick, the all-powerful 'Kingmaker' of the Wars of the Roses. She was first married to Margaret of Anjou's son, Edward, Prince of Wales, and after his death at the battle of Tewkesbury became the much-sought-after bride of Richard of Gloucester. It seems that no one except Richard wanted this marriage, for Anne was hidden in London disguised as a kitchen-maid by her sister Isabel. Isabel's husband was Richard's brother, the Duke of Clarence. After Richard had discovered his reluctant bride, he apparently married her against her will, because an odd document was drawn up to state that even if Anne wished to divorce her husband, all her wealth and possessions would still belong to him.

Within ten years of the marriage, Anne had had a son, but she had lost her sister, the Duke of Clarence had been murdered, king Edward IV had died, his young son Edward V had been murdered, and she had become queen to her husband, Richard III. The coronation arrangements were made so quickly that Anne's dress, cloth of gold on damask, was fitted in two days.

The following year her own child died: an 'unhappy death' is all that is recorded. Anne, worn out with worry, fell an easy victim of tuberculosis. Richard gave her a magnificent funeral but had no time to erect a memorial before his own death at the Battle of Bosworth.

Anne's burial place in Westminster Abbey remains unmarked except for a plaque on the wall in 1960.

Elizabeth of York

Born 1465
Daughter of Edward IV
Married 1486 to Henry VII
Queen until death in 1503. Buried at Westminster
Children:

> *Arthur married for five months to Katherine of Aragon and died aged fifteen*
> *Margaret, who became Queen of Scotland, from whom later British kings were descended*
> *Henry—Henry VIII*
> *Elizabeth, died young*
> *Mary, married first, Louis XII of France; second, Duke of Suffolk, and was the grandmother of Lady Jane Grey*
> *Edmund, died young*
> *Katherine, died young*

Elizabeth, the white rose of York, tall, fair and gentle, a truly English queen, was born at Westminster about 1465. Her father was Edward IV; her mother, Elizabeth Woodville. Before her birth Edward had been told by his astrologers that he would have an heir to the throne. The learned men were more correct than was thought at the time, for after the murder of her two younger brothers in the Tower of London, Elizabeth became her family's heir.

When she married Henry Tudor, the victorious leader of the Lancastrians at the end of the Wars of the Roses, the white rose of York was joined with the red rose of Lancaster to form the Tudor rose, and Elizabeth became queen of Henry VII. The people of England noted with pleasure the real red and white roses blooming on a single bush, feeling that it was a sign of unity and peace after so many years of war. (The rose bush. now called 'York and Lancaster', is still obtainable today.)

Elizabeth's husband had strong ideas, one being about the places in which their children should be born. The first had to be at Winchester,

ELIZABETHA · VXOR
HENRICI · VII ·

Elizabeth of York

the city built by King Arthur, the boy was named after the British king. Henry, possibly because of his own dubious claim to the English throne, was obsessed with his ancestors and had had a great deal of devious research carried out in order to prove his descent from Celtic royalty. In gratitude for the birth of the child, Elizabeth founded a chapel in Winchester Cathedral. For the birth of the second child, she had to be at Westminster, where the ceiling and walls of her room were hung with blue cloth patterned with fleur-de-lis; her bed had a velvet canopy striped with gold and 'garnished with red roses'. The baby was a girl, Margaret, named after Henry's mother, who it was said kept her daughter-in-law under her thumb.

Although Henry did not allow Elizabeth to take part in his own coronation, much to the annoyance of the Yorkists, he gave her a special day of her own, when he watched the ceremony with his mother from a hidden balcony near the pulpit in Westminster Abbey. For this occasion Elizabeth wore her long hair loose down her back and on her head a golden circlet set with pearls and other precious stones; her coronation gown was purple velvet trimmed with ermine bands. On the way to the Abbey her path had been carpeted with striped cloth, but the crowds were so eager to have pieces of it for souvenirs that by the time Elizabeth and her ladies were ready to walk over it, the carpet was in shreds and the queen's procession in disarray.

In spite of the expense lavished on public occasions, Henry was a careful king and Elizabeth had to be a frugal queen. The household accounts show that what little money she had she gave to her penniless sisters, who, although princesses of the house of York, had no dowries to take to their husbands. The most expensive items in the queen's accounts were a clavichord for herself and a parrot. Her dresses were seldom new, for there are mentions of 'gowns being mended, turned and new-bodied', and for her shoes, which apparently only had tin buckles, she paid about twelve pence a pair.

When Elizabeth was about to have her seventh child, which was to be born in the Tower of London – not a very happy choice considering its connections with her murdered brothers – she broke the usual custom of retiring early to the place of the expected birth. Instead, she spent the time visiting all her country houses, including Hampton Court, taking trips on the Thames and enjoying herself with a cheerful Christmas at Richmond. Then, in the middle of January, she and her ladies were rowed down the Thames to the Tower. Elizabeth died there on her thirty-eighth birthday, nine days after the birth of her daughter Katherine. Her coffin, covered in black velvet, rested in the Tower chapel close to the, as yet undiscovered bodies of her two brothers, Edward V and Richard, Duke of York.

After a magnificent funeral given by her husband, Elizabeth was finally buried in the beautiful chapel in Westminster Abbey which Henry had built during his reign. Her effigy can still be seen at the Abbey.

Katherine of Aragon

Born 1585
Daughter of Ferdinand and Isabella of Spain
Married: (i) Arthur, Prince of Wales, 1501
*   (ii) Henry VIII, 1509 (his first wife); queen until she divorced,*
*   1533*
Died 1536. Buried at Peterborough
Children:
Mary, who became Mary I

Katherine, or Catalina as she was called at home in Granada, was the youngest child of Ferdinand and Isabella of Spain. She was only seven years old when her parents finally agreed to help Christopher Columbus on his voyage of discovery to the New World.

Katherine was intelligent and clever, especially in Latin which she could speak and write fluently. When she was sixteen, her prearranged marriage with Arthur, the eldest son of Henry VII and Elizabeth of York, took place in London. Spanish ladies rode side by side in a procession over London Bridge but, unfortunately they had to ride back to back looking as though they were not on speaking terms with each other. The Spanish side-saddles, like little arm chairs, according to one eye-witness, were made to face in one direction and the English side-saddles, of different design, faced in the other.

As Prince and Princess of Wales the young couple had to live near the principality at Ludlow, in Shropshire. It was there that the fifteen-year-old Arthur died only five months later, probably from the plague, leaving Katherine a widow who, from then on, was to be used solely as a political pawn between England and Spain, both seeing which

Katherine of Aragon

would gain the most money from her presence. The wily king Henry VII, her father-in-law, refused to let her go home, as he wanted the rest of her marriage portion paid into his treasury; and he kept the unhappy victim in poverty. Katherine's frequent letters to her father show that she had only two new dresses in five years, that her maids had had none and that she had no money to provide anything for them. Finally it was decided – in order to ensure the receipt of all the marriage portion – that Katherine should marry again. This time it was to be the king's second son Henry, now the heir to the throne. Katherine was not pleased, but when Henry became king, as Henry VIII, a short while later, aged eighteen, and still wanted to marry her, she agreed.

The marriage was in London and, as at her first wedding, Katherine wore her beautiful hair 'at length down her back, almost to her feet'. The following day both king and queen were crowned, and after that to celebrate the event came the cruel form of hunting in which the Tudors delighted – animals were let loose in Westminster Palace to be killed by the court and laid before the queen. Katherine disliked the sport and rarely accompanied Henry, preferring her needlework and more serious relaxations with books and scholars.

During the next eight years Katherine had six children, only one of whom, Mary, survived. As queen, she was so well thought of that she was made regent when Henry was abroad and she supervised the preparations for the country's defence when it was invaded by the Scots – 'busy making standards, banners and badges' she wrote. Her arrangements to ride north at the head of the troops proved unnecessary as the Scots were defeated at the battle of Flodden. Later, Katherine went with Henry on another of his visits to France, when his meeting with the French king took place amid such lavish surroundings that it was known as the Field of the Cloth of Gold.

In London, life was not always easy for a foreign queen and Katherine probably encouraged too many of her countrymen who, no doubt, irritated the English. One 'Evil May Day' as it was called, the young apprentices rioted and attacked the homes of the Spaniards. Henry's Tudor wrath came down upon them and within days boys and men were hanged almost from their own doorposts. It was Katherine who braved her angry husband and pleaded that there should be no more killing.

It was Katherine, too, who revived the interest in gardening which the English seemed to have forgotten during the long wars of the previous reigns. She was horrified to find that it was almost impossible to obtain home-grown carrots and cabbages in London – they were all imported from Holland. Cherries, plums and peaches were rarely available, nor were the ingredients for making a salad, all of which had to be reintroduced. Henry VIII who, according to one historian, 'interfered in all the concerns of his subjects from their religion to their beer-barrels', obligingly imported a gardener from Flanders, and the English returned to a more peaceful occupation.

By the time Katherine was forty and there seemed little hope of her providing the king with a male heir, Henry began to have doubts about the validity of his marriage. His qualms of conscience about being married to his brother's widow were greatly encouraged by the sight of the very attractive young women who attended the queen. He already had one illegitimate son, who had been created Earl of Richmond, and he felt sure that divorce from Katherine and marriage with her lady-in-waiting Anne Boleyn would give him all he wanted. As the deeply religious Katherine would not and could not agree, Henry ruthlessly took matters into his own hands. If the pope as head of the Christian church would not grant him a divorce, then the pope need no longer be head of the Christian church in England. Henry would be that himself – and do as he liked.

His actions towards Katherine would have broken a woman of lesser character. He took away her title of queen, substituting princess-dowager, which Katherine and most of her courageous women refused to recognise; he took away her daughter Mary and made sure that she would never see the girl again. Katherine, after many indignities at court and a farcical trial at which she refused to speak to anyone but the king, was sent off to Buckden Castle in Huntingdon, where she was virtually a prisoner as only those with special passes were supposed to visit her. Katherine suffered it all with patience, even telling her women not to curse the new queen, Anne Boleyn, because the poor girl would need prayers soon enough. Most of her time she spent in needlework and prayer. She ate little, and only what was cooked by her women in the one room she used as bedroom, sittingroom and kitchen: she was obviously afraid that other food might be poisoned. Henry had once threatened to have her executed, to which she had boldly replied that if he could find someone to do it, let him take her if he dared.

After three years and no hopes of seeing her daughter Mary, who was suffering great humiliation at the court of the new queen, Katherine's health broke completely. She was removed to Kimbolton Castle, where she died aged fifty-one. She was buried in Peterborough Cathedral, and remembered with affection by the people of England, who had little time for the woman who had usurped her place. It must have been a genuine affection; William Shakespeare, writing his 'History of Henry VIII' during the reign of Anne Boleyn's daughter Elizabeth, called her 'So good a lady that no tongue could ever pronounce dishonour of her; by my life she never knew harm-doing.'

Anne Boleyn

Born 1507 or earlier
Daughter of Sir Thomas Boleyn
Married Henry VIII, 1533 (his second wife) and queen until beheaded in 1536
Buried at St Peter within the Tower or in Norfolk
Children:
*   Elizabeth, later Elizabeth I*

Anne Boleyn was different in almost every way from Katherine of Aragon. No one seems to have agreed as to whether or not she was beautiful, but luminous black eyes, black hair on which she could sit and a long, slender neck apparently made up for a sallow complexion and one slightly deformed hand. With her liveliness of spirit and absolute enjoyment of life she must have been good company. Exactly when and where she was born have not been agreed either. As she spent most of her youth at Blickling Hall in Norfolk or Hever Castle in Kent, one could easily have been her birthplace. Both were family homes of her father, Sir Thomas Boleyn.

Anne was lucky enough to have a French governess as a child, which made her eagerly sought after, by the time she was fifteen, to go to France as a maid-of-honour to Henry's sister, Mary, when she was married to the king of France. There Anne no doubt learnt enough about court life to prepare her for her return to England, where she became a maid-of-honour to Henry's queen Katherine of Aragon.

At home in England Anne's plans to marry Henry Percy, heir of the Earl of Northumberland, were unexpectedly thwarted by the king himself. Angry and disappointed, Anne took herself off to Hever Castle and even boldly refused to meet Henry when he called to see her father. Later, when it became obvious what Henry's intentions were, Anne's opposition weakened and her ambitions and hopes ran high. Queen

Anne Boleyn

Katherine was middle-aged and no longer likely to give Henry a male heir to the throne. Anne was sure she could provide one for him on the condition that she became his legal wife and thus queen of England.

Henry was bewitched by this 'night crow' as his cardinal Thomas Wolsey unflatteringly described her. Anne and Wolsey had little liking for each other, as Anne blamed him for her early broken engagement and she was afterwards able to achieve revenge in his downfall. Even before Henry's divorce from Katherine, he gave Anne a magnificent apartment at Greenwich where she held her own court; people flocked to pay attention to her in order to secure the king's favour, whatever their real feelings at the sudden elevation of the maid-of-honour. Only the people in the towns and villages remained loyal to the true neglected queen and hated Anne for her arrogance, and later for her cruelty towards the princess, Mary.

Anne went recklessly on her way, self-absorbed enough to enjoy her power. She gambled every night and did not always win; she was extravagant, ordering costly materials for dresses and gowns she designed herself, and which were eagerly copied by the other ladies. She loved hunting, accompanying Henry whenever she could, and her accounts show bills for bow, arrows, shafts and shooting-gloves. Among her pets were a greyhound called Urian for whose killing of a cow Henry had to pay ten shillings; a small dog called Purboy and a linnet in a cage – 'to sing all day'. On one happy occasion she was given a gift of dotterels, a bird now rare in the British Isles due to the fact that others, as well as Anne Boleyn, liked them too much. She ate them – six for Sunday supper, six for Monday dinner and six more for Monday supper.

After a courtship of almost seven years, Henry married her in secret – a marriage which lasted only three years. The coronation was a sumptuous, public affair; the barge carrying his new wife on the Thames was decorated with little flags and bells; the new queen's device was a white crowned falcon bearing the proud words – 'Me and Mine'. A few months later came the blow which heralded the change in Henry's attitude – the expected baby was a girl. She was christened Elizabeth, and Anne, in her disappointment, made sure that Katherine's daughter Mary was reduced to the level of maid-of-honour to serve her tiny step-sister. For a brief while Anne seemed to lose her gaiety, and even took an interest in the new translation of the Bible by William Tyndale and the teaching of the well-known reformer, Hugh Latimer. But when her natural lightheartedness broke through again, it seemed that she walked straight into the trap Henry was preparing for her. She knew he was growing over-attentive to one of her maids-of-honour, Jane Seymour; she knew that mourning should have been worn on the death of the divorced queen Katherine of Aragon and yet she and her ladies dressed in yellow and danced with delight; she knew that Henry would watch jealously every move she made towards any male member of the court – and she still dropped her handkerchief at a tournament where it was picked up and returned to her by one of the contestants.

Henry's rage was uncontrollable or well-assumed – Anne's last baby, a son, had been stillborn, and his hopes were already elsewhere. The Queen, her brother with whom she was accused of having an incestuous relationship, and her supposed lovers, Francis Weston, Henry Norris, William Brereton and Mark Smeaton, were arrested and taken to the Tower of London. There, Anne was put in the care of two women who detested her. In a spirit of vengeance it seemed that everyone, even her own father, turned against her, all being ready to attest to her guilt except the men in the Tower, who refused to incriminate her. Only Smeaton confessed, under torture.

Anne was condemned to death, probably because Henry had no intention of keeping her alive. She was executed on Tower Green – the first woman to be beheaded there – by a sword wielded by the executioner of Calais who had been brought over especially for the purpose. However she may have behaved earlier, Anne met her death with amazing courage and dignity, refusing to be blindfolded so that she could see the executioner. It is said that her body was taken secretly and buried in Norfolk.

Jane Seymour

Born 1509
Daughter of Sir John Seymour
Married Henry VIII, 1536 (his third wife) and was queen until her death
Died 1537. Buried at Windsor
Children:
  Edward, later Edward VI who died aged sixteen

'Jane the Quene', as Jane Seymour signed herself, was Henry VIII's third wife and the only one for whom he showed regret on her death. Jane brought him the son he so much wanted, and in their brief eighteen months of marriage he had hardly had time to grow tired of her or to find fault with her behaviour.

Jane was the eldest of the eight children of Sir John Seymour of Wolf Hall in Wiltshire, and she has come down in history as the gentle, plain, virtuous lady-in-waiting, skilled in needlework and not unintelligent, who briefly became queen of England. That she was skilled in needlework and intelligent has never been questioned, but there some historians ask if she could have been so gentle and virtuous and yet allow the king to pay her such ardent attention while he was married to Anne Boleyn. It was the discovery of the affair between Henry and Jane that caused Anne to lose one of her babies, a boy. Jane certainly had powerful, scheming brothers who would have seen the advantages of having a relative so close to the ear of the king and they could have pushed an unwilling sister. One brother, Edward, became Protector during the reign of Jane's son Edward, and another, Thomas, the Admiral, aspired to the hand of Princess Elizabeth, Anne Boleyn's daughter.

Jane at least acted with more discretion than Anne Boleyn in similar circumstances. She returned Henry's letters and gifts of money to him and, although she lived like a queen in a house outside London, she made sure that she was never left alone with the king until he had worked out how to be rid of his second wife. On the day of Anne's execution, Henry rode off happily to be with Jane, and the pair were married soon afterwards. Jane was received favourably at court, no one actively disputing her position, as both the previous queens were dead. The French ambassador described her as being 'plain, pale and of middle height'; others said that the more magnificently she was dressed the more beautiful she looked. She evidently liked to see her own ladies-in-waiting lavishly dressed, for she insisted that they all wore girdles set with pearls – one young girl who was given a gift of 120 pearls for this purpose was not even then considered to have a rich enough belt to appear before 'Jane the Quene'. No doubt she gave thought to her finery for the coronation – but this Henry kept putting off; there were unfortunate rumours that he had no intention of having her crowned until she had proved her worth by providing him with a son. Jane was not able to do that immediately.

Of her actions or words little is known, and it is likely that she learnt to hold her tongue very early on – her motto was 'Bound to Obey and Serve'. On the one occasion when she tried pleading with her husband,

Jane Seymour

on her knees, as so many of England's queens had done successfully in the past, she was brusquely told not to meddle in the country's affairs 'if she wished to avoid her predecessor's fate'. It was a plea to stop the continuing dissolution of the monasteries and it is not thought that Jane had much time or sympathy for the reformed church of Tyndale, Coverdale, Latimer and Ridley. Martin Luther, the great German reformer of the church, described her quite frankly 'as an enemy of the Gospel.'

It must have been a relief to the uncrowned Jane to know that she was pregnant. Preparations were made at Hampton Court, where Henry had just finished the banqueting hall with the entwined initials of H and J. In October the long-looked-for son arrived, but not without considerable danger to the queen. At one stage, so it was said, the king was asked by the medical attendants whose life they should save, the mother's or the child's: Henry's reply that he could always find another wife was to be expected. The excitement of the christening came only two days later. Jane, wrapped in crimson velvet and propped up on four cushions was carried into the noisy ceremony where trumpets blared and a lengthy ritual had to be endured. Both the princesses, Mary who had been restored to the king's favour through Jane's efforts, and the four-year-old Elizabeth, took their part. That ceremony and the following neglect which Jane suffered when she needed care and attention took their toll. Twelve days later the queen died and Henry, for once, was stricken. He had her body embalmed and buried in St George's Chapel, Windsor, but the wonderful monument he planned was never completed.

Jane was probably in her early thirties at the time of her death. Her ghost is supposed to haunt the staircase at Hampton Court.

Anne of Cleves

Born 1515
Daughter of Duke of Cleves
Married Henry VIII, 1540 (his fourth wife) queen from January to July, when she was divorced
Died 1557. Buried at Westminster
No issue

Fortunate Anne! She married the king and managed to live happily ever after.

Within two months of Jane Seymour's death, Henry began looking for another wife among the princesses of Europe, who had the good sense to value their necks more highly than the uneasy life of a queen of England. The French king was genuinely shocked when asked to bring all the ladies he could muster to Calais so that Henry could view their possibilities. He replied that he could not take 'ladies of noble blood to market as horses were trotted out at a fair'. Henry even wanted to hear all his prospective brides sing, but as no one was prepared to be treated so cheaply, he gave up for the next two years.

The Duke of Cleves was an ardent Protestant, which gave him and his family an added lustre in the eyes of English politicians. He had three daughters, Sybilla, Anna and Amelia. Sybilla was goodlooking, clever and married, and as it seemed likely that Anna and Amelia might take after their sister, tentative enquiries were made in the little duchy of Cleves. Anna had had an excellent education from her mother and although she could not sing – an accomplishment not thought necessary in that part of Europe – nor speak or write any language except her native Dutch, she was a good needlewoman and, presumably, as attractive as her elder sister. When Henry's request for a portrait of her was not granted, he sent over his own court painter, none other than Hans Holbein. Holbein painted what he saw as an artist, a delicate miniature of a girl in her early twenties, placid and contented, wearing the wide, unflattering headdress fashionable in Cleves at the time. He could not show her strong frame and he would not show her pockmarked skin. Henry was delighted and the marriage treaty was drawn up.

Anne, as she was afterwards called, began a leisurely journey to Calais via Dusseldorf, Antwerp, Bruges, Dunkirk and Gravelines. Everything that Anne undertook was unhurried; she enjoyed life immensely, especially her new dresses and jewels and the once-in-a-lifetime honour of becoming queen of England, even if the bridegroom might prove not entirely to her liking. After a delayed voyage across the Channel – that inevitable bad weather again – Anne and her followers arrived at Rochester in Kent on New Year's Eve. There, she was told, a messenger from the king was waiting to give her a New Year gift. Anne was so intent on watching the goings-on of the English out of her window that she hardly noticed the powerful, overweight nobleman who stood beside her. Unfortunately, the nobleman was Henry in disguise; with schoolboy curiosity he had come to view his bride incognito. He was so shattered at the sight of her – and the fact that she had not been impressed at his presence — that he went away, to return with his courtiers and dressed more suitably in purple velvet. After a stilted meeting with the help of interpreters, Henry spoke his mind: everything had been a mistake. The bride was not in the least what he had expected; the tall, big-boned, dark-haired, pockmarked Anne of Cleves was, as he rudely expressed it, 'a great Flanders Mare'. What Anne thought at the first sight of her prospective husband has never been recorded.

Although Henry made every effort to extricate himself from the marriage treaty, the ceremony had to take place. Wishing to inconvenience his bride, he decreed that it should be at eight o'clock in the morning. Anne took her time and was so long at her preparations that the king sent someone to fetch her as he was not used to being kept waiting. Good taste was, apparently, not one of Anne's characteristics; over her own black locks she wore a long fair wig and a circlet of gold 'set about with sprigs of rosemary'; her dress was cloth of gold embroidered very thickly with great flowers of oriental pearls; round her slim waist and neck she wore more jewels. As her dress and those of her ladies were in the Dutch fashion, they were thought strange by the ladies of the English court.

The marriage lasted about five months and during that time Anne endeared herself to the royal children, Catholic Mary, Protestant Elizabeth and baby Edward. Only Henry, it seems, disliked her. 'To me she always seemed a brave lady,' wrote someone at the time, impressed by her kindness, sense of humour and attempts to learn English, as well as her inability to deceive. On the one occasion when she was advised to try to flatter the king and be more loving towards him, she so overacted the part that Henry was angrier than ever.

Henry was quickly growing interested in another lady-in-waiting, the young Katherine Howard, and the queen's lack of affection for him was a good excuse. He decided on a divorce, as even he could find no grounds for an execution, although Anne's retort to him that if she had not been compelled to marry him 'she might have fulfilled her engagement to another man' was bold in the extreme. When the documents for ending the marriage were taken to Anne at Richmond, she fainted in terror thinking it was the warrant for her arrest. She was only too relieved to agree to any terms to end the unwanted marriage. She was to relinquish the title of queen and become 'the king's sister' instead; she was to remain in England and not to marry, but she would have estates of her own and a steady income. Henry was not flattered that she accepted so readily and returned her wedding ring; he could hardly believe that anyone would give him up without a struggle however badly she had been treated.

Anne continued to live at Richmond, where the princess Mary stayed for a few days, and Henry himself had the audacity to come on several occasions, apparently enjoying the brother-and-sister relationship so much that the court was alive with gossip of their re-marriage. Anne's home was a place of contented domesticity, where she took up gardening and cookery. It was reported that 'she has a more joyous countenance than ever' and she put on a new dress every day 'each more wonderful than the last'. When Henry died, she chose to remain in England. At Mary's coronation, after the short reign of Edward VI, she rode in a coach with her favourite stepdaughter, princess Elizabeth, seeming to be the universal aunt and friend of the family.

A few days before she died at Chelsea, aged forty-one, she made her will, leaving something to everyone in her household, money to help with marriages, money to the small children. Her 'best jewel' went to the queen, Mary, and her 'second best jewel' to Elizabeth. Mary gave her a royal funeral and ordered that she was to be buried in Westminster Abbey – the only one of Henry's queens to lie there.

The beautiful miniature of Anne by Hans Holbein can still be seen in the Victoria & Albert Museum.

Katherine Howard

Born?
Daughter of Lord Edmund Howard
Married Henry VIII, 1540 (his fifth wife)
Beheaded 1542. Burial place not known
No issue

Most of Katherine's misfortunes stemmed from the neglect of her childhood. Her father was a poor nobleman, Lord Edmund Howard, who had served his country well as a victorious commander at the battle of Flodden. As is so often the case, he was given little recompense and when he married for love and not for money and had ten children, his family suffered accordingly. When his first wife died, Katherine, whose early years had been spent in the nursery of her cousin, Thomas Culpeper, was sent off to her grandmother, the dowager duchess of Norfolk. There she was left to her own devices and the care of servants, with whom she even had to share a room.

Vivacious, auburn-haired, old for her years, she managed to get into mischief, egged-on by willing companions. Mischief was the music-master, who encouraged her attentions; later it was a Francis Dereham, with whom Katherine secretly exchanged love-tokens, 'silk heartsease' for her, 'sleeves for a shirt' for him. As such tokens in those days meant betrothal or engagement, Katherine was not averse to letting him into her room at night and apparently feasting on strawberries, apples and wine. When such misdemeanours were discovered by the neglectful duchess, Dereham left hurriedly and, so far as is known, became a pirate for a time off the Irish coast; the servants were dismissed and Katherine had the chance to grow into a very attractive, more level-headed young girl.

As Anne Boleyn had been her cousin, it was only natural that Katherine should go to court as a maid-of-honour to the queen, Anne of Cleves, probably soon after all the foreign attendants had been dismissed. It was only a short while after this marriage that Henry VIII noticed the girl among the other ladies. His interest was immediately apparent to court officials who suddenly saw in Katherine a Catholic rival for the Protestant queen, and also someone who could help their own political ambitions. For Henry, she represented an easy solution to an unwanted marriage, and he imagined himself passionately fond of the small, slight figure, his 'rose without a thorn' of the 'winning countenance'. He married her immediately after the divorce and delighted in her company until, out of Katherine's past, rose up the jealousies of people who could not bear to see her elevated to queen of England.

It was while Henry and Katherine were on their way back from a royal progress to the north of England, where Katherine, for reasons best known to herself, had appointed the returned Dereham as her secretary, that word of her past misdeeds was sent to the king. As the evidence piled up, letters from servants, meetings with music-masters, love tokens and recent conversations with her cousin Thomas Culpeper, Henry was forced to call for an investigation. So many people were thought to be trying to hide Katherine's guilt that there was not room for them in the ordinary prisons and they had to be detained elsewhere. Katherine herself was in such a state of terror that it was almost impossible to speak with her. On several occasions when she tried to reach Henry to be with him alone she was dragged back to her room screaming. Henry promised to save her life, a promise which others were determined he should break; and somehow, Katherine never admitted that she could have been engaged to either Dereham or Culpeper – who were later executed. Revelation of a previous contract would probably have secured her a divorce and nothing worse.

Eventually Henry decided that he had no option but to have her beheaded, without allowing her the opportunity of an open trial or freedom to speak for herself. On her arrival at the Tower of London and with only one evening left of life, Katherine asked that the block should be brought to her room so that she could rehearse the horrible event of the next morning.

Katherine Howard was married to Henry for eighteen months and was probably about twenty when she died.

Katherine Parr

Born 1512
Daughter of Sir Thomas Parr
Married: (i) Edward Borough
(ii) John Neville, Lord Latimer
(iii) Henry VIII, 1543 (his sixth wife)
(iv) Sir Thomas Seymour
Queen from 1543 until Henry's death in 1547
Died 1548. Buried at Sudeley Castle, Gloucester
Children:

One daughter by Thomas Seymour

Mary was twenty-seven, Elizabeth ten and Edward six when their father, Henry VIII, decided to give them yet another stepmother – Mary's fifth. The new queen was Katherine Parr who, although only in her early thirties, had been married twice before.

Katherine was one of the three children of Sir William Parr of Kendal Castle, Westmorland. Her mother, plain Maud Green, was a wealthy heiress and when left a young widow had refused all offers of marriage and settled down to devote her time to her small children. Katherine was extremely well-educated in Latin, Greek and other languages, and was highly intelligent – books which she wrote on religious subjects were published after her death; added to these accomplishments was an apparently natural goodness or devotion to duty. Throughout her life she worked for the welfare of others and the one occasion on which she pleased herself ended in tragedy.

As a child Katherine had her horoscope cast by an old woman, who said that she would one day 'sit in the seat of majesty'. This must have impressed the small girl, for when told by her mother not to neglect her work, she replied that her hands were 'ordained to touch crowns and sceptres, not girdles and needles'. In spite of this she was an expert at embroidery and well trained domestically when she was married off at about fourteen to an elderly widower. By the time she was seventeen Katherine was widowed herself, and her mother married her again, to another elderly suitor who survived until she was thirty. Then there appeared on the scene the handsome, swashbuckling figure of Thomas Seymour, one of the brothers of Queen Jane Seymour. He and Katherine fell in love and were planning to marry, when Henry VIII, having executed his second Katherine, began to make advances towards this attractive, intelligent widow who was so different from 'the rose without a thorn'. Henry was past middle-age, grossly fat and suffering from a painful, ulcerated leg which needed expert care: Katherine Parr, with the experience of two previous crotchety old husbands, would be a comforting, unexciting queen.

Katherine was terrified; the loss of her head seemed imminent and she frankly told the king that she would rather be his mistress than his wife. But a sense of duty or the remembrance of the childhood horoscope changed her mind. The handsome Thomas Seymour discreetly disappeared and Katherine and Henry were married at Hampton Court.

Whatever Katherine's real feelings were, she made Henry a devoted wife, nursing him, keeping him amused and taking it upon herself to be a mother to the royal children. She and Mary, so close to each other in age that they could have been sisters, exchanged little booklets on religious subjects; Elizabeth sent translations of French verse for Katherine to approve or correct and young Edward, kept hard at work by his tutors, wrote to his stepmother to say how much he admired her beautiful handwriting and that he was ashamed of his own. It seems possible that Katherine gave him work to copy because there was a marked similarity in the formation of their letters.

It was Katherine's devotion to Protestantism that nearly caused her arrest and execution. Although Henry had broken with the church of

Katherine Parr (*attributed to G. Scrotes, c 1545*)

Rome, he was not so far away from it as to accept the reformed church completely, and he was liable to persecute anyone who did not agree with his own particular brand of religion. Katherine's pleas saved a number of lives, but her brilliant mind found it hard to accept her husband's views on theology. After one such discussion, when Katherine's enthusiasm had allowed her to argue with him, Henry snapped irritably to those around him that things had come to a pretty pass if in his old age he was to be taught by his wife. The queen's enemies were quick to seize the opportunity and worked so successfully on Henry that a list of complaints against her, mainly for supporting the extreme Protestants, and a warrant for her arrest, were duly signed and tucked in the doublet of the lord chancellor. Truth is stranger than fiction – the papers fell unnoticed to the floor of the palace. They were picked up by one of the ladies-in-waiting and immediately taken to Katherine.

Katherine had hysterics – her screams and cries could be heard clearly in Henry's room next door – and after that she took to her bed with a severe illness, real or feigned. She would certainly have known from past experience how to deal with a difficult situation. Henry, ill himself, with no comforting lap on which to place his aching leg, insisted on being taken to her. There Katherine made enough subtle apologies for her 'weak woman's mind' to satisfy her husband's conceit. Later, when the soldiers came to arrest the queen, Henry dismissed them with imperious gestures.

Henry indeed had a high opinion of her, and made her regent when he went to France. On that occasion Katherine signed herself 'Kateryn the Queen Regent. K.P.' The K.P. she always put after her name was perhaps a reminder that she was only Katherine Parr, or else was to distinguish her signature from those of the two previous queens of that name.

Henry died at the age of fifty-six, after being married to Katherine for three years, and to Katherine's surprise she was not made regent for the young king, Edward VI. Instead, back to the court came Thomas Seymour to woo her; Katherine, in a letter, told him how she had always wanted to marry him, only God made her 'renounce her own will and follow Him most willingly'. She and Thomas Seymour were married against opposition in high places, and Katherine's happiness was short-lived. Princess Elizabeth was still in her care and the liberties Seymour took with the fourteen-year-old made Katherine send her and her ladies away from the house. A few months later Katherine had her first baby, a girl, and she herself died within two days of the birth. She was buried at Sudely Castle, Gloucestershire.

Mary I

Born 1516
Daughter of Henry VIII of England and his first wife, Katherine of Aragon
Reigned 1553–58
Married Philip II of Spain, 1554
Died 1558. Buried in Westminster Abbey
No issue

Mary's early childhood was reasonably happy and secure as the only child of Henry VIII and his first wife Katherine of Aragon; she was brought up by her Spanish mother as a devout Roman Catholic and to consider herself as only half English. She was a lively and intelligent child soon displaying a love of music and a deep interest in learning, especially Latin and Greek; she also spoke Spanish, French and a little Italian. By the time she was ten years old, however, it became clear that her mother would not give birth to another child and provide the king with a male heir and Henry decided to divorce Katherine.

There followed a long period of loneliness and grief for Mary. Her mother, rejected and humiliated by the king, was never allowed to see her, and her father, defying the pope to obtain his divorce, abandoned the Roman Catholic faith for the new Protestant religion. At sixteen Mary was faced with first of a succession of five stepmothers; she was pronounced illegitimate and denied the right to succeed to the throne, left alone and insecure to brood over the wrongs done to her mother and herself.

But Mary had inherited a high spirit and strong will from her parents; having a friendly disposition she remained on good terms with most of her stepmothers and being fond of children soon became attached to her younger stepsister and stepbrother, Elizabeth and Edward, taking a keen interest in their education.

Henry VIII died in 1547. His frail young son Edward succeeded him, but only lived a few years longer. Knowing that the Protestant Edward would be succeeded by his Roman Catholic sister Mary, Edward's

Mary I (by Hans Eworth)

advisers had persuaded him to name the sixteen-year-old Lady Jane Grey as his successor. Jane, grand daughter of Henry VIII's sister, had no wish to be queen and during her enforced reign of nine days defied all efforts to make her husband king. After six months of insecurity, Mary, aged thirty-seven and still unmarried, the rightful queen accepted by the people, reluctantly consented to Jane's execution. She was now determined to restore the old religion to England, by force if need be. In a little over four years so many Protestants were burned at the stake that the first queen-regnant in English History gained the title of 'Bloody Mary'.

England also became dismayed and resentful over her choice of a husband. Philip II of Spain was a Catholic and king of a foreign and unfriendly country. Mary and Philip were married in 1554 in Winchester Cathedral (where the stool on which she knelt may still be seen). It was not a happy marriage for Mary herself, let alone the country; Philip showed her little affection and returned to Spain for long periods. Her hopes for a child were disappointed.

There were other worries. Mary was disturbed by rebellion in the country against her and there were plots to replace her on the throne with her step-sister Elizabeth (although Elizabeth took no part in these plans and Mary always showed her sisterly kindness). Mary involved England in a war on the continent, in support of Spain, which ended in a national disaster: the English lost the port of Calais, held since 1347, to the French. Unhappy, insecure and in failing health, Mary finally died in 1558 at the age of forty-two; she gained the reputation, not altogether just, of being one of the most unpleasant and unpopular English sovereigns.

Elizabeth I

Born 1533
Daughter of Henry VIII of England and his second wife, Anne Boleyn
Reigned 1558–1603
Unmarried
Died 1603. Buried at Westminster Abbey

Elizabeth's childhood, like that of her stepsister Mary, suffered from her father's frequent marriages. Her mother, Anne Boleyn, was married for three years and then beheaded, so from an early age Elizabeth learned the dangers of life at court and the need for caution and selfcontrol. She had the companionship of a younger stepbrother, Edward, and the general goodwill of her stepmothers. In particular she came to love and respect Katherine Parr, a woman of culture and literary taste who took a deep and intelligent interest in Elizabeth's education. When Henry VIII died in 1547 Katherine married Sir Thomas Seymour and Elizabeth made her home with them but was soon forced to leave. Rumours spread of the advances Sir Thomas was making to Elizabeth. When his wife died the following year he renewed his attentions, but his obvious ambition to marry a possible heir to the throne was resented and he was executed in 1549.

At this and other times during her youth, Elizabeth was suspected of involvement in plots to supplant her sister on the throne and there were constant attempts to discredit her. Nothing could be proved, and she continued to behave with care and tact – a training useful in later life.

When Mary I died in 1558 Elizabeth was proclaimed queen. Aged twenty-five and the last of the Tudors, she was well received by the country – she was a beautiful young woman of considerable intellect and immense energy – but her position was far from secure. England was divided by fierce religious differences, morale was low after the loss of Calais, French influence over Scotland was feared and finances were almost desperate. Elizabeth, however, possessed caution, wisdom, decision and courage to an uncommon degree; she understood her people, she had the talent to make herself loved by them and she was well advised and well served by her statesmen (in particular Sir William Cecil and his son Robert).

Peace was concluded with France and a religious settlement of compromise successfully carried out. Elizabeth was no fanatic and managed to steer a moderate and sensible course through the difficulties of her reign. As she took the lead, the national sense of security increased and with it came greater prosperity. Elizabeth's court was brilliant, with festivities and finery, the queen herself loved jewels and beautiful clothes, pageants, masques, dancing, hunting and travelling round the country. It was a period of spectacular achievement not only in warfare, discovery and expansion abroad, but also in the arts. Literature and poetry flourished with the work of Shakespeare, Sidney and Spenser; music with the work of Tallis and Byrd. Across the Atlantic Sir Walter Raleigh established a colony in Virginia; the East India Company was

Elizabeth I. The 'Ermine Portrait'. By permission of the Marquess of Salisbury: photograph Courtauld Institute

founded and Sir Francis Drake circumnavigated the globe, returning with £1½ million worth of treasure.

Elizabeth was anxious to avoid war but in time England became involved in fighting on the Continent, lending assistance to the French Protestants and challenging the power of Spain. In 1588 the English, under Drake, defeated the Spanish Armada, a fleet armed to invade the British Isles. It was one of the greatest victories in English naval history.

North of the English border Elizabeth was constantly threatened by plots to restore a Catholic monarchy under her cousin, Mary Stuart, Queen of Scotland, with the support of France. After failures in Scotland, Mary threw herself on Elizabeth's mercy and was imprisoned in England. Many felt that while Mary lived, Elizabeth's life and position were in constant danger; eventually, after long hesitation and heartache, she agreed to have Mary executed, in 1587.

Elizabeth was urged throughout her reign to marry and produce an heir (Philip II of Spain was one of her many suitors), but she refused to commit herself – possibly enjoying the rumours of intrigues with notable men around her – and when she died in 1603 she was succeeded by James VI of Scotland, the son of Mary Stuart.

Elizabeth I was a remarkable woman and an outstanding sovereign – the first, incidentally, to reach her seventieth year. By the end of her reign she had led her country to peace, security and prosperity at home, and to pre-eminence abroad as an independent island challenging the Catholic powers of the Continent. By sheer force of character she gained for herself the credit for the flowering of her time. She could be vain, capricious and wilful, but she was diplomatic, able and well-loved.

Anne of Denmark

Born 1574
Daughter of Frederick II of Denmark and Norway
Married 1589, to James VI of Scotland and became queen of England on his accession to the English throne as James I in 1603
Died 1619. Buried at Westminster
Children:
   Henry, died aged eighteen
   Elizabeth, became queen of Bohemia and was the mother of Sophia, who was the mother of George I

Margaret, died as a baby
Charles, Charles I
Robert, died as a baby
Sophia, died as a baby
Mary, died aged two

If Anne of Denmark had not married James VI of Scotland, it is possible that many of the North Sea oilfields would not belong to Britain today. With Anne came the Orkney and Shetland Islands which, although they had been under Scottish control for some time, were really Danish possessions.

It was said that Anne did not walk until she was nine years old – which made little difference to her dancing ability in later years. Fair-haired, brown-eyed, lively and attractive, at sixteen she left Denmark to marry James of Scotland. Terrible storms, supposed to have been raised by Danish witches, eventually drove her on the Norwegian coast and James, tired of waiting for someone to have the courage to go to her rescue, set off himself. Though highly superstitious and believing in witches, his concern for her safety was greater than his fear, and once landed, he strode to greet her with a resounding kiss. Anne was a little taken aback but soon came to appreciate her shrewd, dry-humoured and extremely slovenly husband. It was an appreciation which deepened with the years as each was able to understand the other's faults. Their first arguments were over their eldest child, Henry, who according to Scottish custom was immediately taken from his mother and given to foster parents. Anne resented this fiercely and did not rest until she was able to take the boy into England with her when James inherited the English throne.

On the death of Elizabeth I, England came to James through his mother Mary, queen of Scots, a descendant of Henry VII, and as they both faced a wider world and an unknown reception, James anxiously asked for some of the former queen's clothes, jewels and ladies to be sent to the border for his wife's benefit. Anne and her two eldest children made a royal progress through the country; Anne loved travel of this kind and once said on leaving Bristol that she had never known what it was to be queen until she went to that city. It was the entertainment that she enjoyed most, and she often took a leading part. At Althorpe on her way to London, the Masque of the Fairies by Ben Jonson, was performed for her in the open air on a warm, midsummer evening in ideal conditions. After

Anne of Denmark (*by Paul van Somer, 1617*)

the coronation, poorly attended owing to an outbreak of the plague, Anne encouraged Ben Jonson to write more masques for the court – the court being, as one writer put it, 'a continued maskerade, where the queen and her ladies, like so many nymphs appeared – and made the night more glorious than the day'. Lacking forest glades, and the weather being not always kind, sets and scenery were designed by the queen's own architect, Inigo Jones. More lasting were his alterations to buildings at Greenwich and Somerset House, then called Denmark House in honour of Anne. Needless to say Anne's debts were enormous.

Besides dancing and plays, Anne enjoyed the hunt; not that she was particularly good at it when it came to shooting a deer with a cross-bow; the only creature that she is recorded as having killed was her husband's much-prized favourite dog, Jewel. James, to everyone's amazement, stopped being angry when he learnt who had committed the dreadful crime and sent his wife a precious jewel and a note saying that it was 'a legacy from his dear, dead dog'. Anne's costume in most of her pictures shows her in hunting clothes – a tall plumed beaver hat, gauntlet gloves, tight bodice and very full padded skirt, a farthingale. These farthingales were the curse of the court, so James said and tried unsuccessfully to ban them after a number of ladies had been stuck in the passage when hurrying to watch the latest masque.

Anne had the sense and intelligence to interfere very little in state affairs although she supported Buckingham and approved of his influence over her husband. She would like to have been made regent when James went to Scotland but she had the ability not to appear hurt when he slighted her. She tried hard to save the life of Sir Walter Raleigh when he was condemned to death on his return from his final disastrous expedition, but she failed, and failed too in her efforts on behalf of Arabella Stewart. Arabella was a young relation of James who crept even closer to the throne when she secretly married William Seymour, younger brother of Edward who, according to the will of Henry VIII, was heir to the throne after his daughter Elizabeth. For this Arabella was imprisoned in the Tower of London, where she died.

Anne's favourite son, Henry, a goodlooking, athletic boy, six feet tall, was taken ill during the preparations for his sister's wedding and died of the plague. Anne was broken-hearted at the loss of both her children, for Elizabeth married a man whom Anne disliked, the Elector Palatine, and went abroad. Young Charles, so unlike his brother, had to try to fill the place of the Prince of Wales and in turn fell ill. His death was forecast –

but in a fit of fury because he obstinately refused to take the medicine prescribed for him, his mother retorted that 'he would live to plague three kingdoms by his wilfulness', possibly she was right.

Anne died aged forty-five after a long illness at Hampton Court.

Henrietta Maria of France

Born 1609
Daughter of Henry IV of France
Married 1625, to Charles I and queen until his execution in 1649
Died 1669 at Colombes near Paris and was buried in the church of St Denis
Children:

> *Charles, died as a baby*
> *Charles, Charles II*
> *Mary, married William II, Prince of Orange*
> *James, Duke of York, later James II*
> *Elizabeth, died at Carisbrooke Castle aged fourteen*
> *Anne, died aged three*
> *Henry, Duke of Gloucester, died aged twenty*
> *Henrietta, called Minette, married the Duke of Orleans*

When Henrietta was about eleven years old and suggestions were being put forward for her marriage, she said that she thought 'a wife ought to have no will but her husband's'. If she had remembered those early words later on when she was married to Charles I, she might have saved herself, her husband and England from the disasters of civil war.

Henrietta was the youngest child of Henry IV of France, one of the great kings, who put his country before his Protestant religion. He was, unfortunately, assassinated five months after Henrietta's birth. His wife, Marie de Medici, naturally brought up the little girl as a Roman Catholic and instilled into her that her faith was the most important factor in her life. When it was proposed that Henrietta should marry the Protestant Charles I, the pope saw the dangers which lay ahead, especially in England where Roman Catholics at that time were deeply mistrusted. His efforts to prevent the marriage failed, and those about Henrietta were so lacking in sound common sense that they sent her to London with a vast following of French attendants who, of course, expected to have their

Henrietta Maria (*attributed to van Dyck, c 1632–5*)

own chapel, a fanatical priest, and a letter from her mother full of advice on leaving home: extremely bad advice, for the enthusiastic sixteen-year-old was encouraged to feel that she was going to England to help the Roman Catholics, a noble project to which her husband was to take second place.

Not surprisingly the first years were unhappy. Henrietta had been spoiled at home and was determined to flaunt her queenly airs, although her right to call herself queen at all was queried when she obstinately refused to be crowned with Charles in Westminster Abbey because the ceremony was against her religious principles. Charles, irritated to begin with, gradually found that he loved her dearly. She was small, dark, lively and 'childishly innocent'; because of her slight stature she delighted in having dwarfs around her, particularly one Jeffery Hudson, who had stepped out of a pie-crust on to the table at a banquet. Henrietta, 'lighthearted, joyous, without sin except those of omission', so it was said, liked to act in court masques, and many of these were written especially to help her learn English, in which she was not too proficient. An ardent Puritan, William Prynne, published a violent article condemning plays, kings, queens and 'women actors': for this allusion to Henrietta, Prynne lost his ears.

Henrietta, remembering her mother's advice, began to dabble in politics, supporting her fellow Catholics by frequent communications with Rome. Her meddling was of little help to her husband, who had enough difficulties of his own in dealing with a Parliament that hardly existed and felt that it should begin to exert more authority. Charles ruled for eleven years without Parliament, struggling to raise money as best he could. When troubles arose in Scotland, Henrietta raised money from her Catholic friends to support the king's armies on the borders, and she certainly influenced Charles in his unwise decision to try to arrest five Members of Parliament in the House of Commons.

When Charles's difficulties came to a head in what was basically a struggle between his High Church belief in the divine right of kings and the more democratic views of the Low Church, the Civil War broke out. Henrietta had not learnt from past experience; she still managed to be rude to some of her husband's most powerful supporters and infuriate others by wanting to bring foreign troops from abroad. Her suggestion that Orkney and Shetland should be given back to the King of Denmark in return for military aid was rejected. No one could say that Henrietta lacked courage and ingenuity. She went abroad herself and raised money to help her husband's cause. On her return to the little town of Bridlington, she had to leap half-dressed out of bed because the Parliamentarians were shelling her arms-laden boat in the harbour. She fled, tore back to rescue her dog and spent the next few hours sheltering in a ditch with her ladies.

As the war turned more and more against Charles and against what Henrietta symbolised, she escaped to the West Country. There she was ill and told Charles's physician, Mayerne, who managed to reach her, that because of her worries she feared one day that she might go mad; Mayerne, who had known her for years and had observed how persistently she had alienated Charles from his people, is reputed to have remarked drily that she need have no fear of that, for in his opinion she had been mad for some time. At Exeter her last child was born, and there Henrietta had to leave her when she fled to France. The baby escaped when she was about two years old, dressed as a ragged little boy in the arms of a beggar woman, one of the queen's ladies. The baby had been told that her name was Pierre and all along the route insisted on telling everyone that she was not Pierre but a princess, and that she did not like her dirty clothes. Henrietta who was overjoyed to see her and rewarded her friend by almost hounding her to death in an effort to convert her to Roman Catholicism, was left penniless and almost starving, as the French royal family were in serious political difficulties themselves.

Even when Charles was imprisoned by the Parliamentarians, Henrietta never gave up hope of being able to help him. His execution in 1649 came as a total shock. Before he died, Charles had been allowed to see Elizabeth and Henry, his two children who had not been able to escape from the country. From Henry he exacted a promise that he would never become a Roman Catholic and never be persuaded to become king while his exiled elder brothers Charles and James were alive. It is difficult to understand how Henrietta had so little regard for her beloved husband's dying wishes for their children. When the fourteen-year-old Henry was allowed to leave England and join his mother in France, she tried to force him to become a Catholic and to enter a Jesuit College. Henry was as stubborn as his mother and held out, backed by a letter from his eldest brother who had asked all the exiled, poverty-stricken English there to give what help they could to the boy. Help he needed because Henrietta turned him out of doors, refusing him food or anywhere to sleep, and sent a message that he was to 'see her face no more'. Her fanaticism mixed ill with her complex character.

When her eldest son returned to England as King Charles II, Henrietta too went back to London for a while. Charles had been the baby whom she had said was so ugly that she was ashamed of him. In England generally there were too many unhappy memories, and her son's uninhibited court was so unlike her own and Charles I's, that she later returned to France. There she died, aged sixty, having been given a too powerful sleeping-draught by her doctor.

Catharine of Braganza

Born 1638
Daughter of John IV of Portugal
Married 1662 to Charles II and queen until his death in 1685
Died 1705 in Portugal. Buried at Belem
No issue

Catharine was Portuguese and when the marriage treaty with Charles II was signed, Portugal became England's earliest ally. Along with Catharine came other benefits – trade with India through Bombay, trade with Brazil and possession of Tangier on the North African coast. For the defence of this port a special regiment was raised in Catharine's honour – the Tangier Regiment of Foot, who afterwards, became the Queen's (Royal West Surrey) Regiment. A portrait of Catharine by the court painter, Lely, shows her seated with a lamb at her feet, and this emblem later became the regiment's crest.

For Catharine, brought up in such seclusion that she had scarcely been out of doors more than ten times in her twenty-five years, there were no benefits. She had little idea of the country or court to which she was going and no knowledge of the language: she and Charles had to speak Spanish to each other. Charles at least showed tact in holding his coronation before his Roman Catholic bride arrived in the country, but dawdled for days before turning up at Portsmouth for the wedding. Catharine's advisers saw that she was accompanied by men of sense, who encouraged her to enter in to the life of the court, and women who would keep themselves in the background. But neither tact nor sense were the king's characteristics where his mistresses were concerned. The desperately unhappy Catharine, so unhappy that she threatened to return to Portugal, found that she was expected to receive and entertain her

Catharine of Braganza (*studio of J. Huysmans*)

husband's women friends. What made the situation worse was the fact that she loved him passionately and knew that he had little time for her.

To his credit, on the loss of her baby Charles nursed her through her illness, and leapt to her defence when suggestions were put forward for divorcing her because of her inability to have children. When that failed, her enemies, notably Titus Oates, an unbelievably dishonest Anglican clergyman, who forged documents in order to discredit the Catholics, brought different accusations against her. She and others were charged with having tried to poison the king, but, as always, Charles was ready to protect her even if he was not able to give her the love she wanted.

More and more Catharine sought her own simple pleasures, tea-drinking, archery, Italian opera and taking the waters at Tunbridge Wells in Kent where she danced every evening with her ladies, usually indoors. Other visitors took the advantage of the bowling green which was 'more soft and smooth than the finest carpet in the world'. Once when staying at Saffron Walden in Essex, Catharine, her ladies and two gentlemen set off in diguise to visit the local fair. Not having any idea of how the ordinary villagers dressed or behaved, the queen's little plump figure in short red petticoats, her dark complexion and foreign accent, soon attracted a crowd, especially when she asked at a stall for 'a pair of yellow stockings for her sweetheart'. The adventure ended with the queen having to run for her horse and the party being chased home by the excited villagers. With such a sense of humour, Catharine deserved greater happiness.

On Charles's death she was far more upset than any of his mistresses; and she continued to live in England on good terms with James II.

At the beginning of James's reign the Protestants hoped to end the Catholic succession by raising a rebellion in the West Country led by Charles II's illegitimate son, the Duke of Monmouth. Ironically, James called out Catharine's regiment who, under Colonel Kirk, savagely put down the revolt and earned themselves the sarcastic nickname of Kirk's Lambs. Monmouth was captured; James unwisely condemned him to death. Catharine pleaded unsuccessfully for his life and watched in dismay the hatred against their common religion which James stirred up by further cruel reprisals. The removal of the Duke of Monmouth left the way clear for other Protestants — William of Orange and his wife, Mary, who managed their accession to the throne without bloodshed.

Under William and Mary, times for the dowager queen and her

friends became difficult, and she eventually returned to Portugal. There Catharine was regent during her brother's illness and when she died, aged sixty-seven, she left her great wealth to him.

Most of the events of the court of Charles and Catharine are vividly recorded in the diaries of John Evelyn and Samuel Pepys.

Anne Hyde

Born 1637
Daughter of Edward Hyde, Lord Clarendon
Married 1660 to James, Duke of York
Died 1671 before his accession. Buried at Westminster
Children:
    Mary, who married William of Orange and became joint sovereign with him —
        William III and Mary II
    Anne, married Prince George of Denmark and became Queen Anne
    Six others who died in infancy.

Anne's father was Edward Hyde, afterwards Earl of Clarendon, Chancellor of the Exchequer. It was in his house in the Strand, without his knowledge, that Anne and James were secretly married in the middle of the night. Edward Hyde was 'struck to the heart' when he heard what had happened and was prepared to send his daughter to the Tower to be executed; Charles II, James's elder brother, laughed and said 'she would do her husband good'.

Of the eight children of the marriage only two, Mary and Anne, survived infancy and they were brought up as Protestants.

Mary of Modena

Born 1658
Daughter of Alphonso IV, Duke of Modena
Married 1673 to James, Duke of York (his second wife) and became queen on his
    accession in 1685 until 1689, when both fled from the country
Died 1718 at St Germains, France, where buried

Mary of Modena (*by W. Wissing, c 1685*)

Children:

Catherine, died as a baby
Isabel, died aged three
Charles, died as a baby
Charlotte, died as a baby
James Francis Edward, Prince of Wales, known as the Old Pretender
Louisa Mary born at St Germains and died aged twenty, of smallpox

Mary Beatrice Anne Margaret Isabel d'Este, nicknamed Eleanor, daughter of the Duke and Duchess of Modena, had every intention of becoming a nun, but at fifteen she was told she was going to England to marry the Duke of York, whose first wife had died two years earlier. Her priest pointed out to her that the marriage would be a yet nobler sacrifice and offering to the Church, for she would be able to convert the English to her faith; so Mary, who had never heard of her prospective husband or his country, agreed to go, but admitted in after years that she burst into tears every time she caught sight of the husband who was old enough to be her father.

Her hopes for England's conversion of course came to nothing; the English in any case had tired of royal brides being sent from overseas for the purpose of doing them good. James eventually lost his throne and was lucky to escape with his head. Even before that, when James and Mary were Duke and Duchess of York, their marriage was unpopular, mainly because it was felt that Mary was hand-in-glove with England's oldest enemy, the King of France.

Mary had been brought up strictly by her mother; she was not allowed sweets or cakes and was 'clipped over the ear' whenever she could not remember her lessons for the day. The treatment had done no harm. She was apparently charming, quickwitted and selfpossessed, qualities she needed when snatched from her secluded unbringing into the wild English court and the arms of a middle-aged man who enjoyed many mistresses. To James's credit, he treated his youthful bride with consideration and soon the difference in their ages did not seem to matter.

Of all the royal palaces, Mary preferred St James, where she insisted on sleeping the night before the coronation and where most of their children had been born. The service of dedication made a great impression on her, although James spent most of the time staring round the building. Mary, tall, slim, dark-haired and dark-eyed, made a regal figure, a heavy purple velvet gown looped with ropes of pearls, over a dress of white and silver brocaded silk, a circlet of gold set with pearls and diamonds on her head. St James's Palace was also the setting of what should have been the happiest day of Mary's life, but it turned out to be one of the worst. After having had three girls and a boy, all of whom had died very young, Mary announced that she was having another baby. Her women and priests declared with conviction that it would be a boy: if so, the rest of the country said, that would mean a Catholic succession – James had long been converted – and what hopes would there be of James's two Protestant daughters, Mary and Anne, coming to the throne? Rumours were put about that there would be no birth, that a child would be smuggled into the queen's room when the time came. Mary drove to St James's Palace and the baby was born. It was a boy and the unbelieving English remained convinced that they had been tricked; it was even suggested that the child had been put into the queen's bed in a warming pan. The matter did not rest there, growing more ominous every day. William of Orange, the husband of James's daughter Mary, was asked to come over to England. Queen Mary found a cruel note pushed into the finger of her gloves casting doubts on her son. Fearing for the life of the child, she rashly decided to run away.

On a stormy December night in 1688, accompanied by a few friends, she and the baby left Whitehall Palace, crossed the Thames in a shallow boat which had been left for them at Horseferry and waited on the other side for a coach and six which was supposed to pick them up. The coach was delayed, and Mary, fearful of being seen by passers-by, hid in the gap between Morton's Gateway of Lambeth Palace and the parish church. Eventually they arrived safely at Gravesend and boarded a boat for Calais. James, as everyone hoped, followed his wife, but not before he had dropped the Great Seal, the sign of his authority, in the Thames.

Life became quiet for Mary, living among the other supporters of her exiled husband, the Jacobites as they were called, she spent most of her time at Chaillot and St Germain. When James died, she and her friends made every effort to have her son proclaimed king as James III and she lived to see his landing in Scotland during the Jacobite Rebellion of 1715. When this failed she helped the fugitive English and Scots who had rallied to him.

Those who knew, Mary Beatrice of Modena loved and liked her, and she lived up to the old maxim that if she could not think of anything pleasant to say about anyone, she should say nothing at all. She died at the age of sixty.

Mary II

Born 1662
Daughter of James II of England and his first wife, Anne Hyde
Married 1677 William, Prince of Orange
Reigned jointly with her husband, William III, 1689–94
Died 1694. Buried at Westminster Abbey
No issue

Mary and her sister Anne were the daughters of James, Duke of York, the brother of Charles II. Although their father was a Roman Catholic the two girls were brought up as Protestants. Mary was born in St James's Palace, London, and spent her early childhood there with her family. Her mother died when she was nine years old and her father remarried two years later. Mary's stepmother, Mary of Modena, was only four years older than herself and the two girls became fond of one another.

As early as 1672 when Mary was ten years old, a marriage was considered for her with William, Prince of Orange, a nephew of Charles II; and five years later the wedding took place. William was twelve years older than his bride, plain and reserved, with a cold, aloof manner, a soldier and politician with no interest in court life and diversion. His personality was a complete contrast to Mary's. She was a beautiful young woman, affectionate, vivacious and charming. To marry William, whom she could not like, at the age of fifteen, and to leave her country, home and friends to live in Holland, was a fearful blow. William was offended by her behaviour and treated her with cold indifference. The marriage did not begin well but Mary's high sense of duty and affectionate nature soon brought her to love and respect her husband deeply. William was unable to return her warmth but seems to have been fond of her.

Mary's arrival in Holland was greeted with enthusiasm – the beauty, piety and sweet disposition of the princess captured the hearts of the Dutch people and, although a foreigner, she became more popular than her husband. The early years of her married life were lonely and Mary sadly found she was unable to bear children, but she liked her new country and developed a lasting affection for its people.

Her father became King of England in 1685, succeeding his brother, Charles II, but the country was uneasy to have a Roman Catholic mon-

Mary II (*after W. Wissing*)

arch. When a son was born to James and his second wife, Mary of Modena, it seemed that a Roman Catholic succession to the throne was firmly established. The general dissatisfaction with James II resulted in a secret plan to restore the Protestant monarchy and place Mary, as the next heir, on the throne. Mary refused to reign alone and the crown was offered jointly to William and herself. William came over to England in 1688 and the change-over (or 'Glorious Revolution' as it was called) was effected without bloodshed; James fled the country and William and Mary were crowned the following year. The monarchy became constitutional and Parliamentary.

Mary continued to lead a lonely life at court, her husband absent for long periods and her relations with her sister Anne unfriendly, but she was as popular in England as she had been in Holland. She interested herself in collecting Chinese porcelain, gardening and architecture.

In 1694 at the age of thirty-two she was taken ill and died. Mary's life had been ruled by devotion to her religious faith and her husband. She was not interested in politics or affairs of state but as queen she did not lack courage or fail to do her duty, and she won the love of her people.

Anne

Born 1665
Second daughter of James II of England and his first wife, Anne Hyde
Married 1683 George, Prince of Denmark
Reigned 1702–14
Died 1714. Buried at Westminster Abbey
Children:
  Anne had seventeen children, but all except one died in early infancy –
  William, Duke of Gloucester, died in 1699 aged eleven

Little is known about Anne's early childhood. Three years younger than her sister, Mary, with whom she was brought up, for a short time she was sent to France for the benefit of her health. When Anne was twelve, Mary married the Prince of Orange and left England, and at the age of sixteen Anne herself was married to Prince George of Denmark. George, goodlooking and amiable, suited Anne well and their marriage was contented, apart from the tragedy of their childlessness: Anne was to bear seventeen children, but twelve died shortly after birth and the others in infancy. Their son, the Duke of Gloucester, only lived for eleven years. The death of her children was a continual grief and Anne also suffered constant bad health. She made several visits to Bath hoping to find a cure through the mineral waters but without success (her example encouraged many others to follow suit and Bath became the most fashionable spa in England during the eighteenth century).

Anne's close friendship with Sarah Jennings, who married John Churchill, first Duke of Marlborough, is well recorded: the Duchess of Marlborough exerted considerable influence over her and the affairs of state.

Anne's father became king in 1685 but was replaced during the Glorious Revolution of 1688 by his daughter, Mary, and her husband, William. Anne, who was also a Protestant, supported the accession of William and Mary and succeeded them to the throne when William III died in 1702. She was the last Stuart sovereign. In later life she and Mary had not been on good terms, weakened by Mary's long absence abroad, Anne's exclusive friendship with the Duchess of Marlborough and quarrels over money.

Anne showered favours on the Marlboroughs when she became queen and the crown was served well by John Churchill. In the war on the Continent England won a series of outstanding victories against the French under his brilliant generalship. After the battle of Blenheim in 1704, Anne gave orders for a palace to be built for the Marlboroughs near Oxford. At this time, however, Sarah Churchill's influence began to wane and she was supplanted in Anne's affections by Abigail Hill, Mrs Masham.

During Anne's time the political parties of Whigs and Tories (later known as Liberals and Conservatives) emerged and there were bitter struggles in Parliament. The most important constitutional act of Anne's reign was the Act of Union in 1707, joining England and Scotland to form Great Britain.

Anne was not clever, or interested in literature, music or art, but her reign was a period of achievement in these fields: for example, the architecture of Sir Christopher Wren and Sir John Vanbrugh; the portraits of Kneller; the writing of Defoe, Swift, Pope, Addison and Steele; the philosophy of Locke and the scientific theories of Newton and Halley.

Anne's health finally broke down and she died in 1714. She was not considered an attractive woman nor one of the great queens, but she has always been remembered for her homely virtues; she loved her country and its institutions, and took her responsibilities seriously.

Anne I, with the Duke of Gloucester (*after G. Kneller, c 1694*)

Sophia Dorothea of Celle

Born 1666
Daughter of Duke of Brunswick-Luneburg
Married 1682 to George of Hanover (later George I). Divorced 1694
Died 1726 at Ahlden
Children:
  George, afterwards George II
  Sophia Dorothea, mother of Frederick the Great of Prussia

Sophia Dorothea was never queen, but as she was the wife of George of Hanover before he came to England to be King George I, and as she was the mother of George II, she deserves to be mentioned.

Sophia was sixteen when she was married to her cousin for political reasons and neither felt the slightest affection for the other. Sophia often hopefully mentioned the possibility of divorce to her father. George was likened to an iceberg and was only interested in the military affairs of Hanover; Sophia was high-spirited, almost frivolous. Bored with the formalities of the Germans and her husband's unfaithfulness, she was easily attracted to a handsome Swedish count, Konigsmark, who frequented the court. Despite warnings from her mother and friends the two wrote numerous letters, tried to meet secretly and finally, it appeared, planned to try to escape from the country together. Konigsmark mysteriously disappeared and was never seen again.

Sophia, only twenty-seven, was given the divorce she wanted on the grounds of desertion, but, not satisfied with that, George had her imprisoned in the castle of Ahlden until she died thirty-two years later. She was never allowed to see her children again and because her son resembled his mother, his father despised him. Thus began the family feuds and hatred among the Hanoverians which lasted for four generations.

Caroline of Anspach

Born 1683
Daughter of John Frederick, Margrave of Brandenburg-Anspach
Married 1705 to George, Prince of Wales and became queen on his accession as
  George II in 1727
Died 1737. Buried at Westminster

Children:

Frederick, Prince of Wales, the father of George III
Anne, who married the Prince of Orange
Amelia
Caroline
George, died as a baby
William, the Duke of Cumberland, called the Butcher of Culloden
Mary, married to Frederick of Hesse-Cassel
Louisa, married the King of Denmark

How many people today would know that the wife of George II was called 'Caroline the Good'? The Georges have so dominated the Hanoverian period in history with the more notorious members of their family, that anything pleasant about them tends to be forgotten. Caroline, in spite of many human failings, was pleasant — 'so charming that she could make anyone love her if she wished'.

She was the daughter of the Margrave John Frederick, ruler of the tiny state of Anspach in the Bavarian highlands. It was a well-governed state where industries and crafts, opera and music were thriving. For Caroline peace and comfort ended too soon, for her father died, her fair, beautiful mother, whom she resembled, was forced to marry again and she and her small brother found themselves a neglected pair. Caroline was too intelligent, too determined and too bored to be idle. At nine years old, it seems, she taught herself to read and write, with the result that in later life her lively letters in French, German and English were full of the strangest spelling and punctuation.

George, her future husband, was another neglected young man, the only son of a father, George of Hanover (later George I of England), who despised him and a mother who was a prisoner in the castle of Ahlden. George wanted to see his prospective bride before committing himself and so in disguise he travelled to Anspach. There, the two immediately liked each other and Caroline was delighted to accept him, having already turned down a much better offer of marriage from the King of Spain. Arguing personally with the priests sent to convert her, she had steadfastly refused to change her religion to suit the Spanish. Later a criticism levelled against her in England was that she was too Low Church.

It was nine years before George's father succeeded to the English

Caroline of Anspach (*studio of Charles Jervas, c 1727*)

throne, inheriting it from his mother, Sophia, the granddaughter of James I. Once Caroline realised that she would be Princess of Wales, and be expected to live in her father-in-law's new kingdom, she set about learning the language and trying to find out something about English life and customs, an attitude in contrast to that of her father-in-law, who had no interest in England; as far as he was concerned it was an intrusion into his life in Hanover. For his cruel treatment of his wife, his many mistresses and his refusal to learn English, he was unpopular from the start. Not many of the English could speak German and court affairs were more often than not conducted in French and Latin.

Caroline's enthusiasm and willingness to go halfway to meet everyone made her and George extremely popular and the sight of the little princesses, Caroline's daughters, bouncing excitedly up and down in their carriage, brought roars of approval from the crowds. There had been no royal family to gaze upon for years and little Anne, Amelia and Caroline grew up to be the most English of Hanoverians. Princess Caroline was apparently the most honest: 'Send for Caroline,' her parents would say in an argument, 'and then we shall know the truth!' Their elder brother, Frederick, did not grow up English. Caroline, on her father-in-law's orders, had had to leave the boy in Hanover to be brought up a German, with the dire results that when he finally came to England some years later he and his parents were strangers. No doubt it satisfied George I, who hated his own son, George, and was not upset by seeing the family feud carried on through another generation.

The princesses Amelia and Caroline were the first royal children to be inoculated against smallpox. Caroline's father had died of the disease and the Princess Anne had been very ill with it; it was typical of Caroline to take to the new idea brought from Turkey by Lady Mary Wortley-Montague. The experiment was carried out first on six condemned prisoners, who obviously had nothing to lose; then on six charity children, who were well-rewarded for their bravery, and finally on the two princesses and the prince in Hanover.

After being in England for thirteen years, Caroline's George became king, as George II, and Caroline was queen — and queen she was, being well able to rule George and having the greatest admiration for and faith in his minister, Robert Walpole. George II confidently left her to manage the affairs of the country as regent while he returned to Hanover, where he still felt far more at home. Caroline enjoyed herself, meeting ministers and politicians and eagerly, in her thirst for knowledge, supporting musicians like Handel, scientists like Newton and Halley, writers like Voltaire, Defoe, Gay and Pope, and being highly amused by the sly digs at her husband in Swift's *Gulliver's Travels*. She also rescued from a dusty cupboard some of Holbein's drawings and had them framed for her sitting-room. Her efforts to improve George's taste in art were less successful: on one occasion she removed the fat, naked Venus from his room while he was abroad and replaced it with Van Dyck's Charles I on horseback, but he furiously demanded to have his favourite back again. 'I like my fat Venus,' he said, and that was that.

Caroline's day began early, interviewing ministers, who stood discreetly behind the door of her bedroom. Then, at nine o'clock she would have breakfast with the children and write letters until George interrupted her so that he could peep through the blinds of the windows to watch the changing of the guard. Sometimes he was in a bad temper – 'Once he stayed about five minutes, snubbed the queen who was drinking chocolate for being always stuffing; snubbed Amelia for not hearing him; Caroline for being grown fat and William for standing awkwardly. Then took the queen out for a walk to be resnubbed in the garden.' The gardens of the various royal residences were in fact Caroline's greatest pleasure. There she let her imagination run wild with informal landscaping and carefully planted trees where she set Merlin's Cave, altogether too German in design for the English idea of a fairy grotto. She added many acres to the royal parks and replanned Kensington Gardens with the Broad Walk and the Great Basin, known as the Round Pond.

At fifty-four, Caroline was taken ill with an internal complaint which she had tried, stoically, to hide for years. In a week she was dead and George was heartbroken; she had been a wonderful companion to him and had even tried to remain on good terms with those mistresses without whom the Hanoverians seemed lost. Caroline was buried in Westminster Abbey and George gave orders that when his own coffin was placed there, the sides of both should be taken away so that they were not separated in death.

Charlotte of Mecklenburg-Strelitz

Born 1744
Daughter of Duke of Mecklenburg-Strelitz
Married 1761 to George III, and queen until her death
Died 1818. Buried at Windsor
Children:

George — George IV
Frederick — Duke of York
William — Duke of Clarence and later William IV
Edward — Duke of Kent and father of Queen Victoria
Ernest — Duke of Cumberland
Augustus — Duke of Sussex
Adolphus — Duke of Cambridge
Octavius — died young
Alfred — died young
Charlotte
Augusta
Elizabeth
Mary
Sophia
Amelia

As Charlotte was only seventeen when she was married, was queen of England for fifty-seven years and was the mother of fifteen children, it seems strange that there is so little by which she is remembered.

George had been king for a year when he decided upon Charlotte, from the tiny duchy of Mecklenburg in Germany, for his bride. She arrived in London for the wedding, which was to be held at ten o'clock at night, after a stormy, ten-day crossing of the Channel when all her attendants were seasick and she amused them by playing the harpsichord. Charlotte was described as being domesticated and sensible, and little more; in looks she was thin, pale, dark-haired with a large mouth and nose and a tendency to chatter continuously in French or German. Nevertheless George liked her, although he had no intention of consulting her on anything outside family affairs, and the two settled down to over half a century of ruling over a kingdom which had not yet come to accept German kings.

Kindly and simple-minded, George earned the nickname of 'Farmer

Charlotte of Mecklenburg-Strelitz (*by I. Cruikshank*)

George' because of his interest in and attempts at agriculture. Charlotte regularly helped her chosen charities, including the silk weavers of Spitalfields, who always seemed to be in need of trade, but she had little time to spare for anything outside her growing family, and there both she and George made unwise, possessive parents. In his mother's eyes the eldest son, later the Prince Regent during his father's recurring insanity, could do no wrong and she even encouraged him in his cruel treatment of his wife. The six princesses, well-brought up, kind and considerate, found that all attempts by young men to marry them were thwarted. The youngest, Amelia, after nine years of pining became dangerously ill. Even then, Charlotte paid little heed and was reluctant to call in another doctor for fear of hurting the feelings of the family physician. While Amelia protested that her death would be due to the 'mis-treatment' of her illness, her mother was attending her own birthday ball. Queen Charlotte's Birthday Ball is still held annually in London for introducing debutantes to society: a peculiar way to remember a queen who gave no lead to society and saw no necessity for giving her bored daughters any experience of the world outside their own family. Needless to say, Amelia, her father's favourite child, died a few months later.

Charlotte had plenty of courage. In old age, when her carriage was surrounded by an angry London mob, fists were shaken in her face and ugly words shouted, she let down the window and addressed those nearest to her: 'I am above seventy years of age; I have been more than fifty years Queen of England and I never was hissed by a mob before.' The people drew back and let her pass.

George III was still mentally ill when Charlotte died, aged seventy-four, at Kew. The old king lived another two years and their unpopular son, the Prince Regent, became the greatly disliked George IV.

Caroline of Brunswick

Born 1768
Daughter of Duke of Brunswick
Married 1795 to George, Prince of Wales
Separated 1796 and not recognised by him as queen on his accession in 1820
Died 1821. Buried in Brunswick
Children:
  Charlotte, who married Leopold of Saxe-Coburg and died aged twenty

I sing the Georges four,
For Providence could stand no more.
Some say that far the worst
Of all the four was George the First.
But yet by some 'tis reckoned,
That worse still was George the Second.
And what mortal ever heard,
Any good of George the Third?
When George the Fourth from earth descended,
Thank God the line of Georges ended.

W. S. Landor.

George III had a number of sons, mostly unstable in character, wild in life style; none had settled down to the respectable family life that would ensure a legitimate line to the throne. More than one had married a woman not recognised by the Act of Settlement. The wife of the eldest son, George, Prince of Wales, was Maria Fitzherbert – a Roman Catholic and for that reason debarred from ever succeeding to the throne. After ten years of secrecy, the Prince threw her over, for a variety of mistresses. His debts grew so enormous that the only way of having them paid was to consent to his father's terms – a marriage with a Protestant princess. The unfortunate girl chosen for this sacrifice was the Prince's cousin, Caroline, daughter of the Duke of Brunswick and George III's sister. Caroline was picked because those who had met her found her vivacious, warm-hearted and very fond of children, and she came from the liveliest court in Germany where none of the stuffiness and gloom usually associated with German royal life was apparent. The instructions given to the twenty-six-year-old princess for her behaviour in England were to keep her opinions to herself, not to gossip with her ladies and to keep her natural lack of seriousness well under control.

The Prince of Wales was glad enough for his father to hold to his side of the bargain, payment of debts, but he had no intention of carrying out his own duties farther than was necessary. With studied cruelty, he sent some of his own women to greet Caroline on her arrival in England, knowing they could be guaranteed to criticise and cause embarrassment to a foreign princess. One of the most unkind tales spread was that Caroline's underwear was of the coarsest material and none too clean. On first seeing her future husband Caroline forgot all the advice she had been given and bluntly spoke the truth: 'I find him very fat and not half as handsome as his portrait.' George called for a glass of brandy and left the room. Nothing could save the marriage after that, and George contrived to humiliate his wife on every possible occasion even to the extent of letting her 'ride badly broken horses and putting spirits in her tea'. They agreed to separate and when their daughter, Charlotte, was born, the child was removed from her mother and it was only through the efforts of the king, George III, that Caroline was given permission to see the baby every week.

Caroline lived alone, attracting to her house writers and artists to whom she proudly showed her vegetable garden, where she tried 'to acquire the honourable name of farmer'. The produce from the garden was sold and the money used for the education and upbringing of nine local orphans. Caroline's love of children had to be satisfied if she was not able to bring up her own child and consequently she adopted the four-month-old son of a poor woman. Ears began to prick, eyes began to pry and probably Caroline's own brand of humour was to blame when someone told the prince that the child was his wife's. The scandal rose to incredible proportions considering that no one took any notice of how George spent his time. Eventually Caroline took herself and the adopted boy abroad to escape the persecution of her husband and his friends, although, since her ill-treatment was a public scandal, she was popular enough with the ordinary people.

George, now the Prince Regent owing to the illness of George III, sent his spies overseas after her to work in her household and to carry tales back to England. These, he hoped, might give him grounds for a divorce, and it has to be admitted that Caroline's wild eccentricities often came up to expectations. The princess Charlotte once said of her parents: 'My mother was bad but she would not have been as bad as she was if my father had not been infinitely worse.' Unfortunately Charlotte, cheerful, popular, outspoken, determined to be ruled by neither parent, died at the age of twenty on the birth of her own dead baby. She was the heir to the throne and had no legitimate cousins.

Caroline's return to England, after some years' absence, on the death of George III to claim her rights as queen, was marked with dismay by the government and renewed efforts to discredit her by her husband now George IV. The usual crowds came out to meet her and gave her a triumphant procession up to London. Perhaps unwisely Caroline refused an offer of money if she would live abroad and give up all her rights as Queen of England. George, furious, brought forward all his spies, all his tales of her friendship and frivolous behaviour overseas and tried to make out that she was not fit to be a queen. Although the whole affair once more became a national issue of enormous interest and was called the 'Trial of Queen Caroline', and questions and speeches were made in the House of Lords, no divorce was granted.

With some degree of confidence Caroline made ready for the final battle, her attendance at the coronation in Westminster Abbey. Here, all the preparations had been made without taking her into account and when she arrived at the Abbey the doors were closed against her and she was refused admittance because she had no ticket. Protests that as she was queen she did not need a ticket were of no avail and when the crowds outside, usually so eager to take her part, began to scoff and laugh, Caroline could take no more. Hurt and humiliated, she drove away.

Three weeks later she was dead, having said that she did not wish to live and wanted to be buried in Brunswick with her parents. But George could not let his hatred of her end there. He sent troops to prevent her coffin from being carried through London and this time the fickle people came to the dead queen's aid. Amid riots and shooting, Caroline's coffin, on which she had wanted the wording 'Here lies Caroline of Brunswick, the injured Queen of England' was borne through the streets and on board ship for her own country.

Adelaide of Saxe-Meiningen

Born 1792
Daughter of Duke of Saxe—Coburg—Meiningen
Married 1818 to William, Duke of Clarence, became queen on his accession as
   William IV in 1830 until his death 1837
Died 1849. Buried at Windsor
Children:
   Charlotte, died day of birth
   Elizabeth, died aged three months

Adelaide was another princess caught up in the rush by the British monarchy to provide legitimate heirs to the throne, especially after the death of Charlotte, daughter of the Prince Regent and Caroline.

There were few princesses in Europe that the sons of George III could marry: most were of the wrong religion, others had families waging local wars. To those seeking a wife for William, Duke of Clarence, the little duchy of Saxe-Meiningen in Germany seemed to have the most advantages, although few were apparent for the bride in such a marriage. Adelaide, at twenty-five, had been brought up simply and sensibly and she had no illusions about what to expect of her bridegroom or her life in England. At home her bedroom, which she shared with her younger sister, was furnished only with chair, table and two beds draped with plain calico curtains and there was no carpet on the floor. The fact that William was twenty-eight years older than she was, had a bachelor home in London and another house in Bushey already filled with his ten illegitimate children of whom he was very fond, did not deter her. If marriage to one of the rather gross, heavy-drinking, loud-swearing sons of George III was the only way to escape from the monotony of life in the duchy, then she would welcome it with open arms.

It almost seemed that William welcomed her with open arms, too. He had been very happy with the actress, Dorothea Jordan, the mother of his children, but the small, graceful, quiet Adelaide appealed to him even more. To everyone's surprise they settled down well together and to everyone's horror, Adelaide made it clear that she intended to love and help William's children, the FitzClarences as they were called for William was still the Duke of Clarence.

William began to eat, drink and swear less. 'You would be surprised at the duke,' someone wrote, 'his wife has entirely reformed him — he is now as quiet and well-behaved as anyone else.' Adelaide reformed his household as well by paying all the bills on time and trying to keep expenses within their budget. She also happily entertained his nautical friends and tried not to be embarrassed by their highly-coloured tales. William had once served in the navy and his excitement knew no bounds when he was given the post of Lord High Admiral — he lost it almost immediately, because in sheer joie de vivre he sailed off at the head of his fleet and forgot to tell anyone where he was going.

The main reason for her marriage, as Adelaide knew well, was to provide William with a legitimate heir and it was a heartbreaking time for her when her baby Elizabeth, the only one of her children to survive birth, died at three months old. After that she lavished all her love on other people's children, especially on her niece, Victoria. Victoria was the daughter of Edward, Duke of Kent, who had been married to Victoria of Saxe-Coburg-Gotha at the same ceremony as William. Adelaide wrote letters to the little girl, never forgetting to send her love to the

'Big Doll' as well and Victoria was sometimes allowed to attend the Queen's parties. At Christmas there would be a tree decorated with golden oranges, nuts and presents. Once Victoria wrote gleefully in her diary, 'We came home at half-past twelve. I was very much amused.'

On the day that William and Adelaide were told that they were king and queen, Adelaide burst into tears, not of joy, because she knew how difficult it would be to control her excitable William. At the best of times no one knew what he would say next and in spring time he was often as mad as a March hare. William wanted to do away with the coronation; it was an unnecessary extravagance – anyone could put the crown on his head, he could do it himself. His brother, George IV, had been wildly extravagant; the whole country was near ruin; there were riots bringing it close to revolution and neither he nor Adelaide wanted to cause difficulties. The coronation took place, but Adelaide paid for her own crown to be made up out of her own jewels. William would gladly have given up other luxuries. He liked walking among his people and enjoyed nothing better than giving visiting kings a lift in his own carriage to their hotels.

As queen, Adelaide had to put up with a good deal of criticism. It was said that her court was a dull, homely affair after that of George IV and her influence over the King was too great when he was trying to bring in the much-needed Reform Bill. Adelaide objected to the Bill on the grounds that it would herald a revolution which would see the end of the British monarchy. The Bill was passed in 1832 and Adelaide was proved wrong. Other reforms of his short reign were in the poor law and local government, and the abolition of slavery. According to other members of the royal family, Adelaide never meddled in politics and never passed an opinion, but she knew better than anyone how too much excitement could unbalance her husband. She persevered quietly, giving support if necessary and tactfully keeping her own German ancestry in the background by patronising English manufacturers – the Spitalfields silk-weavers had an order for twelve dresses – and employing English men and women to work for her.

When William died and the eighteen-year-old Victoria became queen, Adelaide's kindness to her niece was not forgotten. Victoria refused to address her aunt as anything but the 'Queen of England' and gave her permission to take what she liked from the royal apartments. With typical simplicity Adelaide chose a silver cup which William had liked, and the portraits of William and his large family. As a much-loved aunt and stepmother Adelaide passed her time as queen-dowager quietly, travelling by train to different parts of the country and going abroad to try to regain her failing health. In Malta, concerned that there was no church for the English residents, she laid the foundation stone and paid for the building of St Paul's in Valetta. Adelaide, in Australia was named after her. She also set up the King William IV Naval Foundation in memory of the 'Sailor King' (1847). She was living at Bentley Priory in Middlesex when she died at the age of fifty-seven. She was buried at Windsor by the side of William and their baby Elizabeth.

Victoria

Born 1819
Daughter of Edward, Duke of Kent and Princess Victoria of Saxe-Coburg-
  Saalfeld
Reigned 1837–1901
Married 1840 Prince Albert of Saxe-Coburg-Gotha
Died 1901. Buried at Frogmore, Windsor
Children:
  Victoria married Prince Frederick of Prussia, later Frederick III of Prussia
  Edward later Edward VII
  Alice married Prince Louis of Hesse. Great-grandmother of Prince Philip,
    Duke of Edinburgh
  Alfred – Duke of Edinburgh
  Helena married Prince Christian of Schleswig-Holstein
  Louise married Marquis of Lorne
  Arthur – Duke of Connaught
  Leopold – Duke of Albany
  Beatrice married Prince Henry of Battenburg

When Victoria was born in 1819 it seemed unlikely that she would succeed to the throne. Her father, the Duke of Kent, had three older brothers, all married and with hopes of having children, and Victoria was only fifth in line of succession. But during her early childhood her father died and her elderly uncles remained childless. Alexandrina Victoria, as she had been christened, spent the first eighteen years of her life quietly at Kensington Palace. After her father had died, her uncle Leopold of Saxe-Coburg (later King of the Belgians), widower of Princess Charlotte, filled his place to some extent and supervised her education. Her mother, a German princess, relied heavily on her brother Leopold; she spoke no English, disliked her husband's relatives and had been left with little money on his death. By an earlier marriage she had a son and daughter who provided Victoria with great affection and companionship.

Victoria is usually considered one of the most English of queens yet she was half German, and German had been the earliest language she learned from her mother. Her name also had a foreign sound to the English because it was little known in England at the time.

She was a merry and affectionate child, fond of music, dancing, sketching, riding and looking after a little garden of her own. Her life at home was simple and she was taught to dress without ostentation. Her uncle Leopold's choice of husband for her was her cousin, Prince Albert of Saxe-Coburg-Gotha, and he arranged a meeting when Victoria was seventeen; she was anxious to obey her uncle and liked her cousin, but did not wish to marry immediately. So no plans were made for her wedding until four years later when she had been queen for two years.

On her eighteenth birthday in 1837 Victoria came of age, and shortly afterwards the king – her uncle, William IV – died. At five o clock in the morning the Archbishop of Canterbury and the Lord Chamberlain arrived at Kensington Palace to break the news; the new Queen of England received them in her dressing-gown and slippers with a shawl thrown over her shoulders and her hair falling down her back. The English people welcomed her with enthusiasm, her youth and innocence appealing to their sense of chivalry and loyalty to the crown. Victoria was not beautiful, but she was small, graceful and dignified; her manner was pleasant and unaffected. She took her new responsibilities seriously and although inexperienced in affairs of state was wise enough generally to rely on the instruction and paternal care of the Prime Minister, Lord Melbourne – though an imperious streak would show itself on occasions.

She moved with her household to Buckingham Palace and was the first sovereign to occupy the new royal residence in London. She was crowned in Westminster Abbey in 1838, and in 1840 married Prince Albert. The marriage was a success; Albert reciprocated Victoria's deep and lasting love for him and his example and influence gave new weight and stability to her character. Albert was scholarly and conscientious, he had considerable political ability and an informed interest in science and the arts, but he was never popular with the country. The Queen had less intellectual interests than her husband but was a person of strong likes and dislikes: in general her tastes reflected those of the English middle classes.

During the early years of her reign Victoria devoted as much time as possible to her family and to building two new homes, at Osborne and Balmoral. Her first visit to Scotland, in 1842, inspired her with a lifelong regard for the country; that year she was also the first sovereign to travel in a railway train. The Great Exhibition was held in 1851 and the Crystal Palace was erected in Hyde Park for the event: Victoria gave it her support as a demonstration of peace and goodwill among the nations. With the money raised, land was purchased in Kensington for the building of the Victoria & Albert Museum, the Science Museum, the Imperial College of Science and Technology, the Royal College of Music and the Royal Albert Hall.

England was involved in the Crimean War against Russia from 1853 to 1856 and the Queen instituted a new decoration, the Victoria Cross, for acts of conspicuous valour in war. The Indian Mutiny suppressed in 1857, and the Boer Wars of 1881 and 1899–1902 were the principal external disturbances in a long and relatively peaceful reign; with the British Empire in its heyday: Victoria became Empress of India in 1876. Victoria was anxious to avoid war on the continent; she was related to the chief reigning families of Europe, kept in close touch and felt great affection for them which undoubtedly helped to keep England at peace and free from major European troubles. Her large family connected her with the royal houses of Germany, Russia, Sweden, Norway, Denmark, Belgium, Rumania and Greece.

Many political and social reforms were carried out during the reign: legislation which regulated elections to Parliament, the employment of women and children, hours of work, public health and education. Ten prime ministers held office during the reign: Melbourne, Sir Robert Peel, Lord John Russell, Lord Derby, Lord Aberdeen, Lord Palmerston, Benjamin Disraeli, William Gladstone, Lord Rosebery and Lord Salisbury.

Victoria's nine children all married and her first grandchild was born when she was thirty-nine, but two years later Prince Albert died. Shattered, the queen lived in complete seclusion for longer than her country felt was justified. But she was able to celebrate her Golden Jubilee in 1887 with great festivity throughout the country. Her Diamond Jubilee followed in 1897, but her health was beginning to fail and she died in 1901 at the age of eighty-one. She had lived longer than any

English sovereign and hers was the longest reign (63 years) in English history. She was sincerely mourned as one of the greatest British monarchs and her stability and devoted family life were what her country needed.

Alexandra of Denmark

Born 1844

Daughter of King Christian IX of Denmark

Married 1863 to Edward Prince of Wales, and became queen on his accession as
  Edward VII in 1901 until his death 1910

Died 1925. Buried at Windsor.

Children:

  Albert, Duke of Clarence, died from influenza

  George, Duke of York, later George V

  Louise, became the Duchess of Fife

  Victoria

  Maud, became the Queen of Norway

  John, died as a baby

'Why do you always wear a jacket?' asked Queen Victoria of her future daughter-in-law. 'A jacket is so economical,' replied the irrepressible Alexandra. 'You can wear a different skirt with it and I have very few dresses as I have to make them all myself.'

That was Alix, as she was called, the one foreign princess who never seemed a foreigner to the British people. She was loved for her charm and warmheartedness as much as for the beauty and grace which she brought into Victoria's heavily Germanic family.

Alix, daughter of the hard-up Prince Christian of Denmark, came from a happy, simple home where dusting and dressmaking as well as languages and music formed part of her education. Lessons were not to Alix's liking. She preferred listening to the stories of Hans Andersen, who was a frequent visitor, riding, skating, dancing and gymnastics. Even after her marriage to Edward, Prince of Wales, the eldest son of Victoria and Albert, she was capable of performing lightning cartwheels in the drawing-room of her new home.

To Alix and Edward fell the task of livening up London society which had sunk into gloom after the sudden death of Victoria's husband. It was

Alexandra of Denmark (*by L. Fildes*)

with obvious enjoyment that the Prince of Wales and his nineteen-year-old wife took up their duties. Wherever Alix went she was greeted with cheering crowds and some anxious officials, never sure what she would say or do next. 'I go,' being her favourite expression when she had been informed that certain hospitals, people and places were not for her to see — and go she did. At the first Olympic Games to be held in Britain, she was so distressed that the Italian winner of the Marathon had to be disqualified because he collapsed near the finishing line and was picked up by his friends, that she presented him with a special cup of her own. On her visit to Egypt, when sailing up the Nile she was shown the sheep which was to serve as their dinner another day: Alix kept the sheep, alive, and had it sent home to enjoy a happy old age. Her kindliness went deeper than a few eccentric actions, for it was she who arranged for over 300,000 very poor people to enjoy a hot dinner at Queen Victoria's Jubilee celebrations; she planned the first hospital ship for the Boer War, founded the Queen Alexandra Imperial Nursing Service and Alexandra Rose Day. Originally for this all the sellers of flags or roses wore white and were visited by Alexandra in her carriage at their posts.

Queen Victoria grew very fond of her vivacious daughter-in-law and found that underneath the gentle exterior was a character as firm as her own. Although Alix managed nearly always to keep her feelings under control, she suffered bitter resentment for years because of Victoria's support of Prussia against her native Denmark: Prince Albert had always wanted a strong Prussia and had seen his eldest daughter married to the Crown Prince, so to Victoria there was no choice of opinion. While Denmark was at war with Prussia, and her provinces gradually taken over, Alix tightened her lips every time Prussia was mentioned. On one public occasion patriotism overcame her usual reticence and she refused to sail in a ship flying the Prussian flag. Edward, later known as 'the peacemaker', gave Alix his wholehearted support, even when she sided with Russia in their war against Turkey because her sister Dagmar was married to the Russian Emperor, and he managed to steer a tactful course between his mother and his wife.

When Victoria died and Alix and Edward were crowned, the new king showed his respect and affection by paying her the highest honour possible, initiating her into the Order of the Garter. The Order had rarely been used for women since the days of Henry VII.

After a severe illness which followed the birth of Princess Louise in

1867, Alix had to contend with lameness, increasing deafness inherited from her mother and her husband's greater involvement with other women. The lameness she overcame, and she still managed to ride by strapping her saddle on the wrong side; the deafness proved a handicap at social and public functions; but she was able to handle difficult situations with Edward's mistresses with tact and magnanimity. At the time of Edward's last illness she even sent for Mrs Keppel, his most constant companion, knowing that she would wish to see him before he died.

Her good looks remained with her all her life and it was said that she often seemed younger than her daughters with her expressive blue eyes, fair skin and auburn hair. Unpunctuality was her main fault and the clocks at Sandringham were kept fast in the hopes of making her arrive for appointments on time. Alexandra died at Sandringham, her favourite country home.

Mary of Teck

Born 1867
Daughter of Duke of Teck
Married 1893, George, Duke of York and became queen on his accession as George V in 1910, until his death, 1936
Died 1953. Buried at Windsor
Children:
Edward — Edward VIII, abdicated and became the Duke of Windsor
Albert, Duke of York, became George VI
Mary, Princess Royal, married the Earl of Harewood
Henry, Duke of Gloucester
George, Duke of Kent, killed on active service in 1942
John, died aged thirteen

Victoria Mary Augusta Louise Olga Pauline Claudia Agnes, the daughter of the Austrian Duke of Teck and the English princess, Mary Adelaide of Cambridge, was born in Queen Victoria's birthplace, Kensington Palace. As she, too, was descended from George III on her mother's side and was brought up in England, she was the only princess eligible to marry into the royal family. Most of the others were even more closely related to Victoria.

Princess May, as she was called because she was born in that month, was destined to become a future queen and it was arranged that she should marry the Duke of Clarence, eldest son of the Prince of Wales (later Edward VII), who was the eldest son of Queen Victoria and Prince Albert. May, quiet and reserved with a searching, intelligent mind, had been given no special education by her parents, who had not seen any necessity for advanced schooling. But when the impecunious Duke and Duchess of Teck had to spend two years abroad in Italy because their expenses were more than Victoria could face, May swiftly took advantage of the learning it offered and came back to England with a deep appreciation of art and sculpture.

She may have had some doubts about her proposed engagement to the Duke of Clarence. She had known the lively family of the Prince of Wales from childhood and had often found their boisterous behaviour overwhelming. But a few weeks later the Duke of Clarence died suddenly from influenza and the following year May married instead the younger son, George, Duke of York. Queen Victoria wrote of her 'She is really a very dear, good, sensible girl, and very wise – I feel very happy about them.' Fortunately for May, she was happy too. The wedding was in July at St James's Palace and, with past royalty in mind, the future queen had her wedding dress woven by the silk weavers of Spitalfields. The ten bridesmaids wore the white rose of York on their shoulders.

When George came to the throne as George V, May had no wish to be a second Queen Victoria. As Queen Mary she became one of the most regal and dignified, even formidable, figures ever to grace the throne. 'She would make a good factory inspector,' someone said, meaning it as a compliment, so thorough and genuine were her curiosity and interest in everything. Wages, budgeting for small households and the wider issues of the country all claimed her attention, although in politics she discreetly kept in the background. During World War I she organised 'The Queen's Work for Women Fund' which ensured employment for women, and inaugurated Queen Mary's Needlework Guild to provide clothing for those 'who will suffer on account of the war'.

Her own personal interests were just as diverse. She was an expert needlewoman and her magnificent carpet formed of twelve panels showing urns full of delicately coloured flowers was sent on a fundraising tour of America and Canada in 1950. The Canadians bought it for £35,000. 'My gift towards the National Debt,' wrote Queen Mary, happily in her diary. Part of her collection of antiques has been shown at the Victoria & Albert Museum.

Mary of Teck

To many people she is lovingly remembered as a tall, stately figure, always wearing a little toque hat and carrying a rolled umbrella or parasol. She lived to see her grand-daughter married and the births of the first two children. She died at Marlborough House in 1953, at the age of eighty-five.

Elizabeth Bowes-Lyon

Born 1900
Daughter of Claud George Bowes-Lyon, 14th Earl of Strathmore and Kinghorne
Married 1923 to Albert Duke of York and became queen on his accession as George VI, 1936, until his death, 1952
Children:
Elizabeth, later Elizabeth II
Margaret, married Anthony Armstrong-Jones

'Your work is the rent you pay for the room you occupy on earth'; advice from a queen who has dedicated herself with genuine love to the people over whom she and her husband did not expect to rule.

Elizabeth Angela Marguerite, the ninth child of the Earl of Strathmore, was born in Hertfordshire although the main family home was Glamis Castle, Scotland. As a young girl she was told by a gipsy that she would one day 'be a queen and the mother of a queen'; a piece of fortune-telling which was hardly believed even when she met Albert, Duke of York, the shy second son of George V and Queen Mary, and they decided to marry. On seeing his prospective daughter-in-law for the first time George V noted in his diary 'she is a pretty and charming girl and Bertie is a lucky fellow'. Lady Elizabeth Bowes-Lyon's charm and strength of character were to win affection and admiration throughout the world.

The wedding took place in Westminster Abbey in 1923: the future Duchess, followed the example of previous royal brides who helped failing industries, and wore a train of Nottingham lace. In 1926 their first child, Elizabeth, was born and at the beginning of 1927 the young Duke and Duchess were to their dismay sent on a world tour, the main object of which was the first opening in Canberra, Australia, of the Commonwealth Parliament. 'Sweet little Lilibet' as her grandfather,

Elizabeth Bowes-Lyon – wearing Garter sash and star and the Victorian chain (*75th birthday portrait by Norman Parkinson, Camera Press*)

George V, called the baby was only seven months old and spent the next seven months with the King and Queen Mary or the Countess of Strathmore.

Nine years later, after the death of George V in 1936, it became apparent that the Duchess of York might have to assume the role forecast by the gipsy and become queen-consort, for the new King Edward VIII might refuse to remain on the throne. Edward wished to marry an American, Mrs Wallis Simpson, who had been divorced twice and was not acceptable to the British Establishment. His choice lay between abdication and breaking off his proposed marriage. In December 1936 he abdicated. Albert, Duke of York, became a reluctant George VI.

Queen Elizabeth now showed her devotion to her husband and the nation. Without her, George VI would not have developed from the unassuming Duke into the much-loved king who, so soon after his accession, toured the United States of America, and in 1939 helped his people through World War II, visiting factories, docks, and bomb-devastated towns, talking to troops at home and abroad and overcoming his stammer sufficiently to speak on the radio every Christmas.

When he died in 1952 and his daughter became Elizabeth II, it seemed for Queen Elizabeth the Queen-Mother, as she wished to be called, that life had died, too. In the lonely Castle of Mey which she had bought in the north of Scotland, she regained her strength of purpose. She returned to work, to give unbounded pleasure to all who saw her at home, in Canada, America, France, Italy, Africa, Australia and New Zealand; a formidable list of tours which covered the next twenty years.

Her interests are mainly country ones, steeplechasing and horses, fishing and gardening. Her success is due to herself; in her own words, 'I just love people'. 'The Queen-Mum' is an expressive term of endearment.

Elizabeth II

Born 1926
Daughter of George VI and Queen Elizabeth
Married 1947 Philip Mountbatten RN, formerly Prince Philip of Schleswig–Holstein–Sonderburg–Glücksburg (now Duke of Edinburgh)
Ascended the throne 1952
Children:
   Charles, Prince of Wales

Anne married Captain Mark Phillips
Andrew
Edward

Elizabeth was born on 21 April 1926, the elder daughter of the Duke and Duchess of York and not imagined as heiress to the throne. When her uncle Edward VIII became king ten years later, however, her position changed rapidly, for Edward abdicated in order to marry Mrs Wallis Simpson and handed the crown to his younger brother, the Duke of York. So Elizabeth became next in line. She and her sister Margaret had a happy and conventional family upbringing educated at home, although they became more involved in public life. Elizabeth, who was serious and studious with a high sense of duty was particularly close to her father.

In 1945, during the last year of World War II, Princess Elizabeth registered for national service and was officially recorded as 'No 230873. Second Subaltern Elizabeth Alexandra Mary Windsor. Age 18. Eyes blue. Hair brown. Height 5ft 3in'. She had already met Prince Philip – the son of Prince Andrew of Greece and Princess Alice of Battenburg – who was following a career in the Royal Navy. In 1947 they became engaged and were married later that year: royal lavishness was still expected and Princess Elizabeth's wedding dress was embroidered with 10,000 pearls. On his marriage, Prince Philip was created Duke of Edinburgh and invested with the Order of the Garter. A year later their first son, Charles, was born and in 1950 a daughter, Anne.

Princess Elizabeth and Prince Philip took over more public duties as King George VI's health declined and in 1952 it was decided that they should make the lengthy visit to New Zealand and Australia in his stead. Shortly after they had left Britain the king died suddenly and Elizabeth became queen at the age of twenty-six.

She began her reign at a disadvantage: she had not been born heir to the throne and although she was later prepared for the task, the conditions of World War II had given her little opportunity to see kingship working in normal circumstances. But she followed in her father's footsteps as a conscientious, competent, highly respected and well-loved sovereign. The coronation took place on 2 June 1953 – the ceremony being televised for the first time.

Two more sons were born to the queen and Prince Philip and the family life of the royal household has reflected many of the changes in social outlook and habits in Britain since the war. Official visits both at home and abroad have been marked by a growing informality and the queen's children have been educated at public schools. Yet the stability of the monarchy and the pageantry which surrounds it have remained constant, valued by the nation and the commonwealth through periods of international crises and economic insecurity.

Kings and Queens of England

William I	1066–1087	m	Matilda of Flanders	
William II	1087–1100		unmarried	
Henry I	1100–1135	m	(1) Matilda of Scotland	Norman
			(2) Adelicia of Louvain	
Stephen	1135–1154	m	Matilda of Boulogne	
Henry II	1154–1189	m	Eleanor of Aquitaine	
Richard I	1189–1199	m	Berengaria of Navarre	
John	1199–1216	m	(1) Avisa of Gloucester*	
			(2) Isabella of Angoulême	
Henry III	1216–1272	m	Eleanor of Provence	Plantagenet
Edward I	1272–1307	m	(1) Eleanor of Castile	or
			(2) Margaret of France	Angevin
Edward II	1307–1327	m	Isabella of France	
Edward III	1327–1377	m	Philippa of Hainault	
Richard II	1377–1399	m	(1) Anne of Bohemia	
			(2) Isabella of Valois	
Henry IV	1399–1413	m	(1) Mary de Bohun*	
			(2) Joanna of Navarre	Lancaster
Henry V	1413–1422	m	Catherine of Valois	
Henry VI	1422–1461	m	Margaret of Anjou	
Edward IV	1461–1483	m	Elizabeth Woodville	
Edward V	1483–		unmarried	York
Richard III	1483–1485	m	Anne Neville	

Henry VII	1485–1509	m	Elizabeth of York
Henry VIII	1509–1547	m	(1) Katherine of Aragon
			(2) Anne Boleyn
			(3) Jane Seymour
			(4) Anne of Cleves
			(5) Katherine Howard
			(6) Katherine Parr
Edward VI	1547–1553		unmarried
Mary I	1553–1558	m	Philip II of Spain
Elizabeth I	1558–1603		unmarried

⎫
⎬ Tudor
⎭

James I (VI of Scotland)			
	1603–1625	m	Anne of Denmark
Charles I	1625–1649	m	Henrietta Maria of France
Charles II	1649 (restored to the throne 1660)–1685		
		m	Catharine of Braganza
James II	1685–1688	m	(1) Anne Hyde*
			(2) Mary of Modena
William III and			
Mary II	1688–1702		Mary died 1694
Anne	1702–1714	m	Prince George of Denmark

⎫
⎬ Stuart
⎭

George I	1714–1727	m	Sophia Dorothea of Celle*
George II	1727–1760	m	Caroline of Anspach
George III	1760–1820	m	Charlotte of Mecklenberg
George IV	1820–1830	m	Caroline of Brunswick
William IV	1830–1837	m	Adelaide of Saxe-Meiningen
Victoria	1837–1901	m	Prince Albert of Saxe-Coburg

⎫
⎬ Hanover
⎭

Edward VII	1901–1910	m	Alexandra of Denmark

— Saxe-Coburg changed to Windsor

George V	1910–1936	m	Mary of Teck
Edward VIII	1936–		abdicated
George VI	1936–1952	m	Elizabeth Bowes-Lyon
Elizabeth II	1952–	m	Philip Mountbatten

⎫
⎬ Windsor
⎭

* Wife but not queen.

Bibliography

Strickland, A.   Lives of the Queens of England (reprinted 1972)
Greenwood, A. D.   Lives of the Hanoverian Queens of England (1909)
Dictionary of National Biography
Oman, C.   Mary of Modena (1972)
Arkell, R. L.   Caroline of Anspach (1939)
Russell, Lord   Caroline, the Unhappy Queen (1967)
Hopkirk, H. M.   Queen Adelaide (1946)
Gernsheim, A & H   Edward VII and Queen Alexandra (1962)
Tisdall, E.   Unpredictable Queen (Alexandra) (1953)
Pope-Hennessey, J.   Queen Mary 1867–1953 (1959)
Kroll, M.   Sophie, Electress of Hanover (1973)
Sheppard, E.   Memorials of St James's Palace (1894)
Kent, W.   Encyclopaedia of London (1970)
Official Guide to Westminster Abbey (1973)
Wilkinson, F.   The Castles of England (1973)
Laird, D.   Queen Elizabeth The Queen Mother (1966)

All quotations unless otherwise stated are from the above books.

Acknowledgements

Thanks are due to Penelope C. Byrde who contributed the sections on the queens-regnant; Marion Khan for retyping the manuscript with such speed and accuracy; Lambeth Public Library; Epsom and Ewell Public Libraries and my husband without whose constant help and encouragement the book would not have been completed.

All illustrations are from the National Portrait Gallery, London, unless otherwise acknowledged.